CW01022968

**Edizioni R.E.I. France**

All our ebooks can be read on the following devices: computers, eReaders, IOS, android, blackberry, windows, tablets, mobile phones.

**Mantelli - Brown - Kittel - Graf**

Boeing B-29 Superfortress

ISBN 978-2-37297-3571

Edizioni R.E.I. France
www.edizionirei.webnode.com
edizionireifrance@outlook.com

Mantelli - Brown - Kittel - Graf

# Boeing B-29 Superfortress

Edizioni R.E.I. France

# Index

## Boeing B-29 Superfortress

The Boeing B-29 Superfortress (Model 341/345) was a strategic bomber, a four-engine propeller and a middle wing, developed by the US aeronautical company Boeing in the early forties, famous for taking part in the bombing campaign on Japan by the United States Army Air Forces (USAAF) during the Second World War, and for having inaugurated the nuclear age. It was also the largest and heaviest aircraft to have served in the conflict.

A strategic bomber is a heavy aircraft designed to transport large quantities of war loads to a distant target, with the aim of reducing an enemy's ability to sustain the war effort. Unlike tactical bombers, which are used to attack troops and equipment near the front of the battlefield, strategic bombers are designed to penetrate deep into enemy territory to destroy strategic targets such as major cities, factories, and military installations. In addition to strategic bombing, this type of aircraft can still be used for tactical bombing. Only four nations employ strategic nuclear bombers: the United States of America, Russia, India and China.

Born as a high-altitude daytime bomber, it was instead often used for night and low-level bombing attacks on Japan, as well as for the release of the two atomic bombs on Hiroshima and Nagasaki.

The two specimens that operated the atomic bombardment were called "Enola Gay" and "BOCKSCAR".

The B-29 was the single most expensive project in the entire Second World War: its development required investments of three billion dollars.

- It is considered the most effective bomber of the war in every respect as well as the most advanced Allied bomber.

9

Compared to the B-29, none of the major World War II fighter aircraft benefited from such a short time (less than twenty months) between the first prototype flight and the first appearance on enemy territory, regardless of size of the aircraft. In reality, even if particularly advanced from the aerodynamic point of view of the systems and operating concepts, the B-29 was rather conventional in the cell and in construction.

The program for the production of the B-29, outside the training of workers and managers, showed how the aeronautical industry could be equally innovative and flexible enough to quickly build the largest and most advanced aircraft in the world.

The "B-29" program thus allowed the aeronautical industry and the U.S.A. to acquire considerable know-how in the production of complex aircraft. In the specific case, it is not wrong to say that the aeronautical industry probably did more to strengthen the Aviation than the Air Force itself had done.

The total of the orders ordered before the "VJ Day" was 9,052 units, then reduced to 3,965.

During the Second World War, the B-29 dropped 54,917 tons of explosive bombs, 109,068 tons of incendiary bombs and 12,000 mines, with the loss of 377 aircraft, 344 in combat and 37 for other causes.

To date, numerous B-29s, including some still in perfect flight conditions, are stored in aeronautical museums, military bases and private institutions.

In particular, the two aircraft that took part in the atomic bombings on Japan survived: Enola Gay is currently housed in a hangar of the Smithsonian Institution of Washington, DC, while Boxcar, although limited to the fuselage alone, is exhibited inside the USAF Museum at Wright-Patterson Air Base in Dayton, Ohio.

# History

The need for a new generation of strategic bombers to hit targets in Europe or Asia gave rise to the development plan for a very long-haul aircraft.

The first to conceive since the thirties the need for the United States to equip itself with strategic bombers, heavier than the Boeing B-17 Flying Fortress that was still to be put into production, was the divisional general Oscar Westover, commander of the United States Army Air Corps, who died in a plane crash on September 21, 1938. He was succeeded by General Henry H. Arnold who continued his work in favor of a "very heavy" bomber. Boeing began its experiences with very large military aircraft as early as 1934.

The Model 294 was built for the USAAC, a large prototype that took the military name of XB-15. The aircraft was designed to adopt four 1,000 hp engines, but not being available on the date of construction, it was equipped with 850 hp engines that made it too slow and therefore unusable for military purposes. The prototype remained unique and was not built in series. It was then designed an improved aircraft, with high wing, tricycle cart and the announced engines Wright R-3350 Duplex Cyclone from 2000 hp.

The project, named Model 316 was not realized, given the unavailability of the engines.

As committed to the development of the B-17, the Seattle house worked in parallel on a longer-range version of the "flying fortress" with a pressurized cabin.

The experience gained with the 307 Stratoliner, the first pressurized commercial aircraft, led first to the design of the Model 332 of March 1938, a pressurized version of the B-17 and with radial engines Pratt & Whitney R-2180.

Pratt & Whitney radial engines were replaced in the next project, the Model 333A, designed at the end of 1938 to use four twelve-cylinder water-cooled Allison V-1710s, installed in tandem and capable of delivering 1,150 hp, but in February 1939, the Boeing project office, returned to the radial engines with the Model 333B.

The following month, March 1939, a new development was proposed to the air force, Model 334.

The large aircraft, basically a derivative of the Boeing B-17 Flying Fortress, pressurized and with a tricycle landing gear, adopted the new 2,100 HP Wright R-3350 Cyclone engines with General Electric B-11 turbocharger.

The wing had an opening of 120 feet (37 meters), large enough to accommodate fuel for an autonomy of 4,500 miles (8,300 km) and a binary fletching. A new revision of the project led to Model 334A in July 1939, in fact the progenitor of the B-29 family. The prototype no longer had the twin tailing, but used a single large vertical rudder. The wing had been further extended to 135 feet (41 meters) and the engines chosen were the Wright R-3350. The plane was presented to the USAAC and although it did not have resources to finance further studies on the project at the

13

time, Boeing continued to develop at its own risk and with its own funds. A full-size prototype simulacrum was ready by December 1939.

In December 1939, General Arnold was authorized to issue a requirement for a larger aircraft than the B-17 and B-24, a so-called Very Long-Range (VLR) bomber, capable of transporting 20,000 pounds (9,070 kg) of bombs to a distant target 2,667 miles (4,290 km) at a speed of 400 miles per hour (640 km / h). Boeing initially estimated to win the supply, based on the studies already carried out independently and developed the Model 341, a further evolution of the Model 334, a new version that differed from the previous one because it was further larger and equipped with new wing profiles. USAAC formally announced the specifications for the new aircraft on 29 January 1940 and invited the Boeing, Consolidated Aircraft Corporation, Lockheed and Douglas Aircraft Company to supply.

The new bomber had to transport 16,000 pounds (7,250 kg) of bombs for 5,333 miles (8,600 km) at an average speed of 400 mph (644 km / h), ensuring a minimum of comfort on board for those who had to travel, given the circumstances, for twelve to fourteen hours in a row. Boeing responded by proposing the Model 345 on May 11, 1940, in competition with a Consolidated project, whose Model 33 later became the B-32 Dominator, with Lockheed, which introduced the Lockheed XB-30, and the Douglas Aircraft Company who introduced the Douglas XB-31. The Model 345 was the further evolution of the Model 341 and differed from the predecessor for a new landing gear, with double wheels and legs that retracted in the engine gondolas and not in the wing, and for the adoption of remote-controlled defensive towers, in practice the main features of the future B-29. The technical and industrial risk was very high: the only prototype would have cost much more than it could have been allocated, and mass production would have potentially brought many of the resources available for collapse; all this without counting the technical and engineering effort that, at the time of the project (1940), consisted of a real challenge. Douglas and Lockheed soon abandoned the competition and Boeing on 24 August 1940 received an order for two flying prototypes, to which the designation XB-29 was assigned, plus a static test cell. The order was modified on December 14, with the addition of a third flying specimen.

Consolidated continued to work on its Modell 33, which was taken into account by the Air Corps, as a reserve in case of problems with the Boeing project.

In May 1941, Boeing was assigned an initial order for the production of 14 pre-production aircraft, plus 250 production bombers. The necessary appropriations arrived with the entry into the war of the USA following the attack of Pearl Harbor on 7 December 1941: the program obtained three billion dollars for the development and the same amount for mass production. The order was increased to 500 aircraft in January 1942 and then to 1,500 bombers. The combat aircraft that resulted, after an evolution passed through the same structure of the B-17 (and through some considerable redesign, with speeds estimated even higher than 640 km / h), had twice the weight, thickness of the coating external, power, autonomy and payload compared to the predecessor, with unit costs of an order of magnitude higher than those of the Fortress, which already cost as much as a dozen of Curtiss P-40: the outlay of $ 639.188 1942 for each plane is equivalent to a unit price of 3 billion dollars today, which makes the B-29 the most expensive weapon system of the entire second world war. The first prototype made its inaugural flight from Boeing Field, Seattle on September 21, 1942.

Because of the extremely innovative design of the aircraft, the complexity of the required requirements and the great pressure on the production lines, the initial phases of the project were very troubled. The second prototype, unlike the first that was unarmed, was equipped with a defensive armament system of Sperry that used turrets for remote-controlled machine-guns, for which they used periscopes.

The first flight of this second prototype took place on December 30, 1942 and was interrupted due to a serious fire to an engine. On February 18, 1943, the same plane crashed during its second test flight, as another fire of the engine this time spread to the wing and the plane fell on a factory placed at the edge of the runway. In the accident the entire crew of 10 men was killed and 20 more victims were added to the victims among the people involved on the ground. The modifications to the production aircraft were so frequent and so fast, that at the beginning of 1944 the B-29s flew from production lines directly to modification workshops to undergo extensive reworking necessary to incorporate the latest design variants. The Air Force ran the modification workshops fighting with the breadth of the required rework and the lack of hangar able to accommodate the B-29, all combined with the frost that slowed down the work. The situation was such that at the end of 1943, although 100 aircraft had been delivered from the production lines, only 15% were usable.

This state of affairs caused an intervention by General Henry "Hap" Arnold who was responsible for solving the problem. Staff were sent from the factory production lines to the modification centers to speed up the work and have enough aircraft to equip the first bombing group in what was called the "Battle of Kansas". 150 planes were modified in the six weeks between March 10 and April 15, 1944.

It was then almost a year before having aircraft able to operate reliably.

The construction process of the B-29 was complex and four main assembly factories were involved: two plants operated by Boeing in Renton in Washington State and in

Wichita in Kansas, a Bell Aircraft Corporation plant in Marietta, Georgia ("Bell -Atlanta "), and a Martin plant in Omaha in Nebraska (" Martin-Omaha ").

Thousands of subcontractors were involved in the project.

In June 1943 the delivery of the 14 pre-series units began and the Air Force units immediately began operating with the new bomber. The first series aircraft, on the other hand, were delivered in the autumn of the same year.

At the end of 1943 the military command decided not to use this type of aircraft in Europe, but to concentrate the intervention of the B-29 against Japanese targets, an operation in which the very long autonomy of the B-29 would prove to be very useful.

The production of the B-29 reached 2,527 units before the next model, the B-29A, was introduced.

The latter had a wingspan of 12 inches (30 cm) higher than the previous type, engines Wright R 3350-57 or 59, also with star cylinders, a reduced capacity of the tanks and a front dorsal tower with four arms instead of two. This type of turret had been mounted, even on the last specimens produced by B-29, which lacked the 20 mm cannon of the turret in the tail sector.

Before May 1946, when production of B-29 A ceased, 1,119 such specimens were built.

With the decline of the Japanese air power it was possible to eliminate the defensive armament and its auxiliary equipment from the B-29, with the exception of the tail turrets. This allowed the offensive load to be greatly increased. This expedient proved so happy that since then the type with the designation B-29B has been produced, of which 311 specimens were built.

# Technique

The B-29 was a heavy bombardment device, with a monoplane and entirely metallic structure, with a constant cylindrical section fuselage of about 70% of the length, conceived for high altitudes, four-engine and overall conventional in shape, even if realized with technologies avant-garde: shielded systems, remote-controlled weapons, pressurized cabin and an electrical and hydraulic system of unprecedented complexity. The aircraft had a total of seven generators: two on each external engine, one on each internal engine and one APU. The cell represented a radical innovation with respect to the traditions of Boeing, and involved the use of new metal alloys and new construction techniques. Where the B-17 had adopted a tubular beam structure for their wings, a technique dating back to the Monomail of 1930, the thin wing of the B-29 and the massive flaps that were mounted there required a completely new structure, a structure that would have indicated the way for future developments in the jet age.

The low resistance wing was revolutionary for the time and took the project name 117. The wing profile used generated twice the lift of the B-17 wing.

General LeMay said: "It was the wing that made the airplane". Moving the B-29 were four air-cooled Wright R-3350 engines, with 18 cylinders in the twin-star configuration in tandem, and a total displacement of 55 liters.

The engine was equipped with a stagnant self-oil tank congruous with the general proportions of the giant that supported 322 liters.

They had a take-off power of 2,200 hp, but a General Electric turbocharger system allowed 25,000 feet (7,600 meters) to re-establish a power of as much as 2,300 hp, in an emergency, developing a power horse for each pound of engine weight. The engine, however, became the most common cause of serious accidents and therefore of concern for maintainers.

Over time, the Wright R-3350 became a reliable "draft horse", comparing it to other large piston engines, but the first models were plagued by dangerous reliability problems, mostly caused by the rush to use the B-29 in the shortest possible time in operating theaters.

The engine had an impressive power-to-weight ratio, but this performance was achieved at the expense of its durability. To make matters worse, the engine covers were designed by Boeing too close to the mechanics, as the improvement of aerodynamics was favored. The first design of the motor flabels used for cooling caused vibrations and dangerous flutter phenomena in the open position in most of the flight envelope conditions.

The 18 cylinders of the radial engine, arranged on two compact stars, one front and one rear, showed a worrying tendency of the star of the rear cylinders to overheat due to the insufficient flow of cooling air, consequence of the design choices made on the fairings. To mitigate the inconvenience some changes were introduced to get more cooling at low speeds and the planes were sent in a hurry in the Pacific theater in 1944. The decision was not wise, as the initial tactics of employment of the "Super Forces", they planned to operate with the maximum load and from airports with high ground temperatures. Under these conditions, the engines overheated regularly, particularly during the ascent after take-off. The exhaust valves were dilated and the air-fuel mixture acted like an oxyacetylene torch on the valve stems. When these were destroyed, the valves were drawn into the cylinders and caught fire.

The resulting fire, not being in the front part, but in the rear part of the engine, was not turned off by the fire extinguishers on board and became impossible to control.

In addition, an auxiliary engine component, made of high magnesium alloys and installed at the rear, often caught fire and produced such intense heat as to overcome the flame retardant coating in the engine compartment.

In these conditions, the fire spread to the wing spar, in no more than 90 seconds, causing the aircraft wing to break with catastrophic effects. In addition to being subject to fires for various structural and cooling problems, the Wright R-3350 engines were inadequate for the size of the machine: 8,800 HP were not enough for the 60 gross tons of the Superfortress, and the operational career performed in the heat torrid tropical latitudes could only worsen the efforts. The R-3350 would need several years of tuning in more than what was granted. He entered the service still not completely developed, becoming the nightmare of the mechanics and a concern for the pilots, especially when it was a matter of taking off at full load from a short track in crushed coral. The problem was not solved until the more powerful Pratt & Whitney R-4360 "Wasp Major" were adopted with the B-29D / B-50 program, which came too late for World War II.

As a temporary solution, appendages were placed on propeller blades to divert more refrigerant air into the engine cooling openings. The openings were also equipped with deflectors to direct a specific airflow to the engine exhaust valves.

The amount of oil for the valves was increased and asbestos gaskets were placed on the engine to prevent oil leaks. The airplanes were subjected to very thorough prior checks, in which the possible presence of out-of-place engine valves was checked.

The top five cylinders were replaced more frequently (every 25 hours of engine operation) and the entire engine was replaced every 75 hours of operation. The pilots, including those of the present day at the controls of the Fifi of the Commemorative Air Force, the last B-29 still able to fly, describe the flight after take-off as a desperate struggle to gain speed, while in other aircraft, in general the flight after take-off is an effort to reach altitude. Radial motors need adequate air flow for cooling and failure to reach adequate speed in time could result in engine failure and fire risk.

Evolution of the B-29 engines:

- XB-29 - Wright engine R-3350-13 - 2,200 hp (1,600 kW)
- B-29 - Wright engine R-3350-23 – 2,230 hp (1,660 kW)
- B-29A - Wright engine R-3350-23 – 2,230 hp (1,660 kW)
- XB-39 - Allison V-3420-11 engine – 3,042 hp (2,268 kW)
- XB-44 - P & W engine R-4360-33 – 3,042 hp (2,268 kW)

- B-50A - P & W engine R-4360-35 – 3,549 hp (2,646 kW)
- B-50D - P & W engine R-4360-35 – 3,549 hp (2,646 kW)

The crew, for the first time in a bomber, could enjoy the comfort of a complete pressurization.

The B-29 pressurization system was developed by Garrett AiResearch and was the first ever built for a Allied series bomber.

The Boeing had previously built the 307 Stratoliner, which was the first commercial airliner with a fully pressurized cab and was produced in only ten units. Unlike planes of the same era, such as the Junkers Ju 86P, to which the pressurized cab was added at a later date, the B-29 was designed from the beginning with a pressurization system.

The front and cockpit were pressurized, as was the back.

The designers had to make the decision whether to leave the bomb chamber unpressurized, or put the entire fuselage under pressure, which would have created the need to depressurize the aircraft each time before the bombs were launched. The decision was made to design a long tunnel above the two bomb chambers, so that the crew members could move from the front to the rear, both pressurized like the tunnel.

The bomb compartment remained at ambient pressure.

Photo of the interior of the pressurized rear cabin of the B-29, June 1944

A further project was initially known as XB-29D, and was capable of remedying the major shortage of the B-29: the power-to-weight ratio. This was remedied with the 3,500 hp engines developed and used also, but in six copies, the B-36 Peacemaker.

The development will be dragged for a long time, with the use of a more resistant alloy and a tail higher than 1.7 meters. Eventually an almost totally different aircraft came out, called the B-50. This aircraft from over 600 km / h reached roughly the speed performance originally required, but also consumed something more than the less powerful B-29.

With these new-generation engines, the Wright R-4360, one of the 3,970 B-29s built, has been tested since 1944. The end of the war, however, meant that the order for 200 B-29D was reduced to 60, and that the project was not simply reworked, but was redesigned with lighter and more resistant alloys. Then a B-50 will circumnavigate the globe (with refueling in flight), and the entry into service will be done around 1948. But for the time the B-50 was considered a 'medium' bomber and the use of the great atomic bombs of the time required that the aircraft should be lifted from the ground to let them enter, in the bomb compartment. Produced in about 400 specimens, it was not used in Korea, but was used above all as a reconnaissance and aero refueler.

Characteristic of the B-29 was also the different arrangement of the cuffs compared to the other bombers. In fact, instead of being at the center between the two pilots, there were three groups of four handcuffs available to the pilot (on his left), and four available to the co-pilot (on his right).

Finally, four available to the navigator; see in the following image the four levers with blue knob available for pilot, co-pilot and orange for the navigator.

## Armament

The B-29 was able to fly up to an altitude of 40,000 feet (12,200 meters) at speeds up to 350 knots (650 km / h). These performances represented his best defense, as the Japanese fighters of the time could barely reach such odds and few could approach the B-29s, if they had been waiting at the right altitude. Only the heaviest anti-aircraft weapons could hit them, and since throughout the Second World War the axle forces had no artillery with proximity quill, striking or damaging these bombers from the ground was almost impossible.

The revolutionary Central Fire Control System - CFCS (centralized system for fire control) was designed for the B-29. On the plane there were four remote controlled turrets, each armed with two machine guns .30 cal M1919.

The weapons were controlled by four machine-gunners who helped each other with four analog computers from General Electric. Each machine gunner, with the exception of the tail machine, could control more than one defensive position at the same time. One of the machine-gunners found a place above the Norden pointing system in the nose and the other three were placed in pressurized compartments at the back of the fuselage, which had bubble windows. The gunner of the upper rear post was the gunner known as "Central Fire Control gunner", whose task was to coordinate the work of the other three weapons officers avoiding confusion during the battle.

The CFCS systems had highly advanced analog computers at the time, capable of compensating for the shot taking into account the speed of the B-29, the speed and weight of the target, gravity, temperature and humidity.

Thanks to this aid, the useful shot of the B-29 .30 caliber machine guns had an effective range of 1,000 yd (914 meters), twice the useful shooting range reached with the hand-held machine guns on the B-17 Flying Fortress.

Ventral turret armed with two M1919 machine guns, .50 caliber and remote controlled.

The tail machine gunner could only control his weapons (two M1919s, in the first production units, a 20 mm M2 cannon) and the rear lower turret.

After World War II, the turret towers were equipped with their own APG-15 targeting radar.

At the beginning of 1945, with a change in the mode of employment, passing from that of high altitude daytime bomber to low-altitude night bomber, according to reports, General LeMay ordered the removal of most of the defensive armament and of the systems of pointing away from his B-29s, so they could take on more fuel and bombs.

As an effect of these requests, Bell Marietta (BM) produced a series of 311 B-29B without aiming systems and turrets, armed with the only turret, in which two Browning caliber .50 guns and a M2 cannon were placed, plus the APG-15 pointing radar.

This armament was immediately modified in three M1919 machine guns.

This version was also equipped with an improved "Eagle" APQ-7 radar for targeting bombing even in bad weather.

This radar was installed at the bottom of the fuselage, covered by an aerodynamic profile radome.

Most of these aircraft were assigned to the 315th Bomb Wing, based on Northwest Field, on the island of Guam.

The lack of a front turret as in the case of the B-17G made the B-29 more vulnerable to actions in the anterior sector, but its speed made such a danger negligible; the glazing was extensive but the snout offered very little protection from the enemy fire not having front armor. Even so it was an exceptional aircraft, with a coating thickness doubled compared to the already respectable B-17, and global and high altitude capabilities such as to exceed those of the existing fighter and bomber.

# Use

The pre-war doctrine of the U.S. Army Air Corps predicted that the bombers. Grouped in non-escorted formations were used for strategic attacks carried out at high altitude, primarily on airports and objectives related to the aeronautical industry. In April 1943 the generals Arnold and Marshall agreed on a "plan for the correct use of the B-29 against Japan" and promoted an acceleration of the production of the aircraft. At that time only two prototypes had already flown in the context of a program that was still called a "three billion dollar venture" by its critics and its detractors.

The plan initially drafted (summer 1943) by the commander of the South Pacific Pacific Air Force planed to concentrate attacks on the fuel refineries of Borneo and Sumatra. which had constituted the primary goal of the Japanese invasion at the beginning of the conflict.

In contrast to this conception, the commander of the U.S.A.F., General Henry H. Arnold, constituted the 20th Air Force, with a centralized organization to strategically employ the new bombers and concentrate the action against Japan; subtracting it from the control of the sector commanders, on April 4, 1944, he personally took command from Washington.

On April 6, 1944 was finally approved the incendiary offensive on Japan and at the same time were prepared for the 20th Bomber Command, then main department of the 20th Air Force, five bases in India and four in China (where over 700,000 Chinese workers took part in the construction ).

The Chengdu region was eventually preferred to that of Guilin to avoid having to train 50 Chinese divisions to protect the bases against Japanese land attacks.

This project was extremely expensive, as there were no land connections between India and China and all the materials necessary for the operation of the advanced bases had to be transported by air crossing over the Himalayas through transport aircraft, or with the same B-29, using some specimens to which the protections and weapons were removed to transform them into airplanes for the transport of fuel.

The first B-29 arrived in Kuangchan in China on April 24, 1944, but the initial sortie of the B-29 took place on June 5, 1944 on Bangkok, departing from Indian bases.

77 of the 98 B-29s departed from the bases in India and were sent to bomb the Bangkok railway workshops in Thailand. Five B-29s were lost due to technical reasons.

The first base job in China was followed on June 15-16, 1944, with an attack on Yawata steel plants in the southern part of Japan by 47 B-29. It was the first bombardment on the Japanese islands by the Doolittle raid of April 1942. In this mission there were the first combat losses of B-29, with one of the planes destroyed by Japanese fighters on the ground after an emergency landing in China, one lost due to the anti-aircraft fire on Yawata, and another plane, the Stockett's Rocket (named after Captain Marvin M. Stockett, the aircraft commander) who disappeared after taking off from Chakulia in India. The raid caused little damage to the target, with only a bomb that hit the facilities and practically exhausted the fuel reserves of the Chengdu bases, causing operations to slow down until the stocks were reconstituted. Five bases were then set up on the Marianne islands in Guam, Saipan and Tinian, operational since November 1944, sufficient to operate around 900 aircraft. Since October 29, five bombings have been designed to gain experience in order to make the bases fully operational; four on Truk (1,290 km south-east) and one on Iwo Jima 1,210 km north, with few aircraft for action and negligible results.

Initially, the Japanese carried out contrast actions on Saipan with twin-engine fighters and bombers taken off from Iwo Jima and the Pagali islands. Against the B-29 was also adopted by the Japanese tactics to intentionally launch with fighter planes against the bombers looking for the collision. The first example of this technique was recorded during the August 20 raid on Yawata steel plants. Sergeant Shigeo Nobe of the 4th Sentai intentionally flew with his Kawasaki Ki-45 against a B-29; the debris projected by the explosion severely damaged another B-29 that crashed.

The two US losses were the B-29 serial number B-29-10-BW 42-6334 Gertrude C with commander Colonel Robert Clinksale and the B-29 serial number B-29-15-BW 42-6368 Calamity Sue with commander captain Ornell Stauffer, both of 486th BG. Many of these aircraft were destroyed in this type of attack in the following months.

Although the term "Kamikaze" is used to identify this type of attack, the word is not used by the Japanese historiography that distinguishes between suicide attacks on ships and air combat of this type, not necessarily suicides.

In addition to the logistical problems associated with operations departing from China, the B-29s could only reach a limited part of Japan from those bases. The solution to this problem was the conquest of the Marianne Islands that would have brought goals like Tokyo, 2,400 km away, within the radius of "super-fortresses".

It was therefore decided in December 1943 to conquer the Marianas. Saipan was invaded by US forces on June 15, 1944, and despite a Japanese naval counterattack leading to the Battle of the Philippine Sea and bitter fighting on the ground, the island was made safe on July 9th. The battle of Guam and the battle of Tinian followed, which led to the possession of the three islands for the month of August. Work on the islands began immediately with the aim of building airports capable of hosting the B-29s. Operations began even before the end of fighting on the islands.

A total of five large airports were built, including two on the flat Tinian island, one in Saipan and two in Guam. Each was large enough to accommodate a bomb wing consisting of four bomb groups, with a total of 180 B-29 per airport.

These bases, which could be supplied by ship unlike those in China, were not vulnerable to ground attack by the Japanese army and became the launching point for major air strikes against Japan conducted in the last year of the war. The first B-29 arrived in Saipan on October 12, 1944, even before the completion of the air base and the first combat mission launched by the Marianne bases started on October 28, 1944, consisting of 14 B-29s attacking the base of Japanese submarines of Truk Atoll. On November 24, 1944, 111 B-29 attacked for the first time the Musashino engine factory in the Tokyo area: an action hampered by bad weather and by enemy hunting and - consequently - poor results and some losses.

The first actions with baseline departures in the Pacific were neither very effective nor frequent, mainly because they were hampered by adverse weather, with substantial cloud cover on Japan; moreover, the first experience was made with the jet stream (jet stream) at high altitude (jet streams consist of one from a set of very strong winds, up to 320 km/h, on fronts of 300 450 km, located around the earth at the altitude of the troposphere).

The climb to 9.100 meters and above often created considerable problems for the R-3350 and, at the same time, the winds in the tail, sometimes, during the return flight, brought the speed compared to the ground at over 700 km / h, hindering the maneuvers of approach to the bases of departure. Engine problems were reduced after Boeing suggested starting low-altitude missions, thereby consuming a significant amount of fuel before making the climb to operating altitude.

Because of the uncertain or stormy weather, none of the eleven priority targets were destroyed in the first 2,000 sorties. One third of the actions involved the Musashino area, which was only destroyed by 4%. As of January 1, 1945, 750 B-29 overseas departments were operational. Although less known, the Starvation Operation (hunger) consisting of a program to detach anti-aircraft mines from the planes, carried out by the B-29 against the main naval routes and the Japanese ports, seriously compromised the Japanese ability to continue the war operations.

The B-29s were withdrawn from the airports in China towards the end of January 1945. During the period of use of these aircraft departing from China and India, missions were carried out against many targets throughout Southeast Asia, but the gradual transfer was decided. of the entire fleet to the new bases in the Marianne islands.

The last mission departing from India was launched on March 29, 1945. Probably the most famous B-29 is the Enola Gay, which launched the "Little Boy" atomic bomb on Hiroshima on August 6, 1945. Bockscar, another B-29, dropped "Fat Man" on Nagasaki three days later.

These two actions, together with the Soviet invasion of Manchuria on 9 August 1945, forced Japan to surrender and officially end the Second World War.

Both planes used for nuclear bombing were chosen and then modified from aircraft assembled in the Omaha plant, in what would become the Offutt Air Force Base.

After the surrender of Japan, the V-J Day, the B-29 were used for other purposes.

A certain number supplied the prisoners of war captured by the Japanese with food, medicines and other basic necessities, parachuting loads of rations in the camps where the Japanese kept the prisoners in conditions that needed urgent interventions, well before the evacuation.

In September 1945, a long-haul flight was completed for propaganda purposes: generals Barney M. Giles, Curtis LeMay and Emmett O'Donnell, Jr. drove three modified B-29s from Hokkaidō Chitose Air Base to the Chicago Municipal Airport, continuing to Washington, DC, the longest non-stop flight ever achieved at that time by Army Air Force aircraft and the first non-stop flight of history between Japan and the United States of America.

Two months later, Colonel Clarence S. Irvine made the command of another modified B-29, named Pacusan Dreamboat, another record-breaking flight that broke the world record, covering the distance between Guam and Washington without a stop. , for a total of 12,740 km in 35 hours with a takeoff weight of 70,000 kg. Although conceived for other theaters and only briefly evaluated in England, the B-29 was mainly used in the Second World War only in the Pacific theater.

The prototype YB-29-BW 41-36393, from the name Hobo Queen, was seen to make a stop in several British airports, it is thought for an operation of "disinformation" of the Germans, with the idea of making believe that the "superhardness" it would also have been used in Europe. After a two-week period, the plane was sent to India to join the 462nd Bomb Group. After the war, some squadrons of the Bomber Command of the Royal Air Force were equipped with some B-29 lent by USAF reserves. When they were in service with the RAF, the aircraft took the name of Washington B.1 and remained in service from March 1950, until the last one was returned at the beginning of 1954, being replaced by the first "V" series bombers British -bomber.

The bombers were employed in 34,000 sorties with 5 tons of bombs each, confirming the formidable load capacity of the bomber.

During the night actions, in which the planes flew at low altitude almost without defensive weapons and with a small crew, it was possible to load over 6 tons of M69 napalm bombs, consisting of 38 2.7 kg submunitions that opened at about 1,500 meters of quota.

Despite the reputation of substantial invincibility of the B-29, the campaign ended with the loss of about 500 airplanes, mostly due to accidents, with over 3,000 victims among the crews, a fairly high price for a device that was produced in 3,970 pieces .

The B-29 was used in the 1950-1953 period in the Korean War. At first, the bomber was used in strategic bombing day missions and the few North Korean strategic industries and targets were quickly reduced to rubble. In 1950, however, the MiG-15 "Fagot" Soviet jet fighters appeared, aircraft specifically designed to knock down the B-29s, and after the loss of 28 bombers, the Americans changed the technique of using the B-29s, restricting their use only at night bombardments and against supply lines. The B-29 also launched the radio-controlled bombs "Razon" and "Tarzon", in occasion of precision attacks against dams and main bridges, such as those on the Yalu River. The "super-fortresses" were soon made obsolete by the development of jet-powered fighters. With the entry into service of the gigantic Convair B-36, the B-29 was reclassified as an average bomber in the newly established United States Air Force.

The B-50 Superfortress variant, initially designated B-29D, had sufficient performance to cover auxiliary roles such as search and rescue, electronic espionage and even tanker.

The B-29D was replaced in the early 1950s by the Boeing B-47 Stratojet, which was in turn replaced by the Boeing B-52 Stratofortress.

The last B-29s were radiated from service in the mid-sixties after a total of 3,970 built specimens.

# Fire bombing

In the second half of 1944, the scientists of the U.S.A.A.F. they had examined the possibilities that could be offered on a large scale of incendiary bombardments on the cities of Japan.

The direction of N.D.R.C. (National Defense Research Committee) transmitted to the upper command of the Army Air Force a reminder that contained this prediction: *"a preliminary calculation of the necessary forces and foreseeable damage of the war potential that would be caused by incendiary bombardments on Japanese cities, indicates that these can represent the best solution for a strategic air war throughout the present campaign, and probably an opportunity to cause maximum damage to the enemy with the least effort.The preventive calculations of the economic damage provided indicate that the bombing of Japanese cities with incendiary means can have at least five times the efficiency, with the same tonnage, a precision bombardment of strategic objectives determined according to the methods followed in the war in Europe ".*

With napalm it was no longer necessary to directly bombard the stations because the incendiary liquid spread over a large area, higher than that affected by the explosion of a high-potential bomb. Furthermore, the napalm burned the vegetation used to mask the posts, penetrated the shelters and smothered or burned those that were there. The effectiveness was very high, without trace of wounds or burns. died simply because of the lack of oxygen so that often people were dead in the open. Napalm was used for the first time in March 1944 by the B-24s of the 7th A.F. on Ponape, with the launch of about 20 tons of M-69 bombs. Other attacks followed during the landings at Tinian and Guam in 1944. The turning point in the use of the B-29 occurred with the appointment of General Curtis E. LeMay on July 4, 1944, at the head of the 20th Bomb Group; on January 20, 1945, LeMay also assumed the command of the 21st Bomber Command based in Guam.

- The first bombing of the new type on Japan was carried out by the 21st Bomber Command on 6 January 1945 in Nagoya with the release of 138 tons of incendiary weapons.
- On February 4, 1945, followed the first incendiary bombing on Kobe.
- February 25, 1945 took place the first night bombing on Tokyo, with 450 tons of incendiary bombs launched 172 B-29; on the occasion, the loss of only three planes had to be lamented.
- On 9 -10 March 1945, the 21st Bomber Command carried out an attack with 325 B-29, of which 279 acted on the target with 2,086 tons of bombs (including 1,753 tons of M-69) which destroyed 15 square miles of the urban area of Tokyo, ie four times the area devastated in Hiroshima.

It was the same area already destroyed during the earthquake, and the subsequent fires, in 1923.
The estimated deaths were 83,703 and the injured 40,918, but the reality was more than 100,000 dead, where only four aircraft did not return among the attackers.
Regarding the civilian victims of this attack, it reflects what was declared in the Sixties by the then Defense Secretary McNamara: *"The sense of proportion should be a guide in war ... There is a rule that should not be killed 100,000 civilians in one night ... What changes actions making them moral if you win and immoral if you lose the war? "*

- From 11 to 18 March 1945, in a paroxysm of flames and fire, four attacks followed:
- March 11 on Nagoya
- March 13 on Osaka
- March 16th on Kobe
- On March 18, a second attack on Nagoya.

These operations led to the exhaustion of the equipment of incendiary bombs in the base of the Marianne islands, and therefore in the following two months only incendiary attacks were carried out, on April 15th on Kawasaki and on May 25-26 on Tokyo. The most contrasted action was that on Tokyo of 25-26 May with 498 B-29 in action, 464 on the target, 26 lost for Japanese action, equal to 5.6% with 254 human losses, and 100 damaged planes, equal to 21.3% of the total.

- Results: 18.9 square miles of urban fabric destroyed by flames and 17 attacked shooters. After adequate stocks of bombs were set up, the incendiary raids that destroyed all Japanese cities, except Kyoto and smaller cities, such as Hiroshima and Nagasaki, resumed.

In these actions 50% M-69 bombs were used and the remaining 50% were incendiary weapons or high explosive bombs. It is not altogether absurd to assume that, if the availability of napalm bombs of the 21st Bomber Command had not been insufficient, it would have been possible to obtain the surrender of Japan without the use of the two atomic bombs (according to the estimate of the United States Strategic Bombing Survey, Pacific War - Washington 1/7/1946, Japan would in any case surrender in November 1945 without the use of atomic weapons).

# The napalm

In May 1940 the formation of the National Defense Reaserch Committee (NDRC, Committee for Scientific Research for Defense) was proposed, formally established on June 15, 1940 under the pressure of events.

In September 1941, General Arnold requested the president of the NDRC to initiate the study and development of devices that could replace magnesium incendiary bombs, due to the severe scarcity of this element.

In October 1941, a study group became operational at Harvard University, while the NDRC entered into a contract with the Development Office of the Standard Oil Company for research into incendiary bombs using petroleum derivatives. Both groups directed their research towards the development of a mixture that used compressed gas as incendiary material, following the example of Great Britain which had gelatinized gasoline with natural rubber (a product that is no longer obtainable after the occupation of the East Indies from the Japanese side).

A study conducted by Harvard University on the gelatinization of gasoline with soap with aluminum soap and coconuts, led to the discovery of napalm. With some improvements the production process was defined, which allowed to obtain a granular powder soap from which a petrol jelly was obtained by simple mixture at room temperature.

The first practical application was made with the 31.5 kg M-47 bombs made by the Chemical Warfare Services, triggered by percussion quills and using a central burst tube filled with explosives.

In the spring of 1942, the M-47 bombs were enhanced with a central tube containing a TNT core surrounded by white phosphorus.

A further development was then constituted by the incendiary bombs with ejected charge from the back, studied by the Standard Oil. Charged to petrol jelly and equipped with timings to allow the device to pierce the roof and the underlying slabs, they could project the incendiary charge over a large area. Large-scale tests led to the standardization of the incendiary bombs on the M-69 model, equipped with new primers, whose petrol gelatin charge was contained in a hexagonal tube of 66 mm and 267 mm long.

At the same time, Standard Oil developed the quill with adjustable retarder and other improvements. M-69 bombs were then tested against rural buildings destined for demolition, near the Jefferson polygon, in Indiana; since the results were strongly questioned by those who considered these buildings much more easily incendable than buildings in Germany and Japan, with the collaboration of architects who had worked in the two countries, typical German and Japanese houses were built.

Particularly significant for the definition of the details of use of the weapon were the Dugway, Utah tests, carried out from May 17 to July 16 1943 on a group of twelve "Japanese" houses for two families and six "German" houses, totally furnished with original or reproduced furniture. Furniture and rugs and other household accessories from residents of Japanese origin were taken from Hawaii and the west coast, while furniture that realistically reproduced the German or Japanese one was made "ad hoc" to make the little "Little Tokyos".

Firemen teams were tasked with extinguishing fires using traditional methods employed in Japan.

These tests highlighted the superiority of the M-69 bombs on all the other types and, on the basis of these experiences, the plan of attack was incendiary to the Japanese cities, with the support of the NDRC personnel, towards the end of 1943. From 'autumn 1943, it was established that the incendiary bombs had to be produced in containers (having the same ballistic characteristics of large-caliber bombs), destined to open at a height of a few thousand feet. At the end of 1943, 10,000 containers were required for use by the 20th A.F. in China; the bombs were produced by the Chemical Warfare Service in the winter of 1943-1944 and by the private industry starting in March 1945. At the end of March 1945, 30 million M-69 bombs were produced.

# Technical features

## Dimensions and weights

- Length: 30.20 meters
- Wingspan: 43.00 meters
- Height: 8.50 meters
- Wing area: 161.60 m2
- Empty weight: 33,800 Kg
- Load weight: 54,000 Kg
- Maximum takeoff weight: 60.560 Kg
- Crew: 11 men:
  - Pilot
  - Copilot
  - Bomber
  - Flight engineer
  - Navigator
  - Radio Operator
  - Radar operator
  - Right-wing artillery
  - Left artillery
  - Central artillery
  - Tail artillery.

## Propulsion

- Engine: 4 Wright R-3350-23 Duplex Cyclone 18-cylinder radials each with two turbochargers
- Power: 2,200 hp (1,641 kW) each

## Performance

- Maximum speed: 576 km / h at 7,600 meters
- Cruise speed: 350 km / h
- Stall speed: 170 km / h
- Ascent speed: 4.6 m / sec
- Autonomy: 4,000-9,500 km
- Tangency: 10,200 meters

## Fuel

- 31,030 liters on the first models, made in four wing tanks.
- 36,140 liters after the installation of additional tanks in the central section of the wing.
- 26,450 liters only in operating conditions, if semi-permanent fuel tanks have been removed.

## Armament

Four remote controlled towers:

- Two under the fuselage - each tower housed two Browning M2 12.7 mm machine guns with 500-1,000 strokes each.
- Two above the fuselage - each tower housed two Browning M2 12.7 mm machine guns with 500-1,000 strokes each.
- A turret controlled by a stand-alone machine gun - three weapon options were available: a 20mm Hispanic-Bendix AN-M2 cannon and two 12.7mm Browning machine guns or three 12.7mm Browning machine guns or two 12.7 mm machine guns

Some aircraft also had an upper front turret equipped with four machine guns.

**Bombs**

- Up to 9,000 kg divided as follows:
- 20 from 250 kg or
- 40 from 250 kg or
- 18 of 500 kg or
- 8 of 1,000 kg.

During the Second World War, the B-29 completed over 20,000 missions, with an estimated 180,000 tons of dropped bombs.
Each aircraft required more than thirteen tons of aluminum, half a tonne of copper, 600,000 rivets, 15 km of wiring and 3 km of pipes.

# Wright R-3350 engine

The Wright R-3350 Duplex Cyclone was an air-cooled twin-cylinder 18-cylinder radial aeronautical engine, produced in the 1940s by the US company Curtiss-Wright Corporation. The Duplex Cyclone was one of the most powerful radial engines produced in the United States. Its development began before the outbreak of World War II, but the engine required a long period of maturation before being used on the Boeing B-29 Superfortress bomber, just before the end of the conflict. After the war the engine was sufficiently mature to become the main engine used in civil aircraft projects, particularly in its Turbo-compound version.

The code R-3350 identifies the model based on its displacement in cubic inches, about 3,350 in$^3$.

In 1927 the Wright Aeronautical began production of its most representative engine, the Cyclone, which manned several aircraft during the 1930s.

In 1929 the company merged with Curtiss giving rise to Curtiss-Wright. After this merger, a more powerful version of this engine was developed that could reach 1,000 hp (746 kW).

From this project came the Wright R-1820 Cyclone 9 whose production began in 1935 and which will become one of the most used engines in the thirties and during the Second World War. In the same period the competitor Pratt & Whitney began the development of a new bigger and much more powerful engine based on its equally famous R-1830 Wasp engine.

The new model adopted a double-star configuration, with cylinders arranged on a double row instead of a single one like its predecessor, which could easily compete in terms of power delivered with the R-1820.

In 1935, therefore, the Curtiss-Wright decided to undertake a similar development starting from the mechanics of the Cyclone.

The R-3350-57

At the end two projects were also characterized by a double star and short-stroke cylinders: a 14-cylinder engine that will be developed in the R-2600 engine and an 18-cylinder engine that will become the R-3350.
The first R-3350 was completed in May 1937.
It immediately proved to be an engine with a very strong character. The development continued slowly due to the complexity of the engine and the greater attention paid to the 14-cylinder version.
The engine did not conduct flight tests until 1941, ie only after the XB-19 aircraft replaced the Allison V-3240 engines with the Wright R-3350s.
Things changed drastically when a US Army Air Force (USAAF) issued a specification for the development of a long-range strategic bomber capable of flying from the United States to Germany with an offensive load of 900 kg

(2,000). lb). Although as small as the Bomber D project, which will materialize in the XB-19 prototype, the new aircraft required engines with comparable power.

Wright GR-3350

When three of the four preliminary designs submitted adopted the R-3350 engine it became clear that the latter was the engine of the future of the USAAF and therefore all the necessary efforts were made to start it quickly in the series production phase. flights the latest development of the new program for this new bomber, the XB-29, the prototype of the Boeing B-29 Superfortress.

The engine, however, continued to possess a non-constant yield and also showed a worrying tendency to overheating.

To overcome these drawbacks, a series of numerous modifications began to be introduced, directly on the production line of the aircraft, to improve low-speed cooling.

In 1944 the aircraft were sent to the war theater of the Pacific War, but it became evident that the problems of overheating had not been solved so much that some aircraft were burnt after take-off.

The initial versions of the R-3350 were equipped with carburetors that created mixing problems.

These problems in turn caused an inadequate distribution of the mixture.

At the end of the Second World War an injection fuel system was introduced and immediately the engine reliability increased.

These engines became the favorites in large civil aircraft projects such as the Lockheed Constellation and the Douglas DC-7. Subsequently, to meet the demands of the civil market, a device was designed to further improve performance in order to be able to contain fuel consumption, the Turbo-Compound system. A turbo-compound system is a technological solution that can be used on internal combustion piston engines to partially recover the energy contained in the exhaust gases.

It was developed from the second half of the forties by the US aircraft engine manufacturer Wright Aeronautical Division.

In the turbocharger (a system used in aeronautical engines to deliver the available power at sea level), the cylinders discharge the combustion gases into a common collector with two outlets; one through the wastegate valve which, when opened, regulates the maximum supercharging pressure and one that feeds the turbine. When the valve is open, the pressure in the manifold is practically equal to the atmospheric pressure, while when the valve is closed, the exhaust gases are forced to pass through the turbine (of the "jet" type) which exploits the pressure drop to move the compressor, but it also negatively influences the emptying of the cylinders during the unloading phase.

The Wright R-3350, equipped with a Turbo-Compound device

In the turbo-compound, however, the discharges of the cylinders are directly connected to the turbine (in this case of the "action type") that works with a negligible pressure drop, transforming the kinetic energy of the exhaust gases into mechanical work, not introducing deleterious overpressures to the exhaust and taking advantage, as the altitude increases, of the increasing pressure jump between the one in the combustion chamber (which remains practically constant) and the atmospheric one (which decreases with altitude).

In a turbo-compound engine, the turbine is generally mechanically connected to the driving shaft by means of a suitable series of reduction gears, but an electric version has also been studied in which the turbine drives a generator which can power an electric motor.

The energy thus recovered saves between 2.5 and 5% of fuel, depending on the configuration; the use of this system is particularly indicated in the case of engines that operate for a long time at their maximum power. Starting from

1942, the Wright Aeronautical Division began to study in the aeronautical field a system for recovering the power otherwise lost in the exhaust gases of the piston engines.

Since 1946, the U.S. Navy subsidized this research that led, in 1950, to the first production model, the Wright R-3350. In this engine, at the opening of the exhaust valves, the pressure in the combustion chamber rapidly collapses from about 14 atmospheres (200 psi) to atmospheric pressure, leaving the exhaust gases to sonic speed (which for that average temperature corresponds to approx. 670 m/s). The three turbines installed (which rotated up to 19,000 revolutions per minute) allowed for this engine a gain of 410 kW (about 550 hp) at the maximum continuous power regime.

With this system an additional 20% of energy was recovered, which otherwise would have been lost in heat.

In addition to the Wright R-3350, the turbo compound was also developed on other aircraft engines such as the Napier Nomad, the Rolls-Royce Crecy, and the Allison V-1710, although for the latter two did not go beyond the stadium of prototype. The simultaneous development of turboprop engines and turbojet quickly supplanted the increasingly complex piston engines and with them the turbo-compound versions.

From this moment on, moreover, the reliability of the engine had been further increased with a MTBO (maximum time before a revision) placed at 3,500 hours and an SFC (specific fuel consumption) of the order of 243 g/kWh.

Versions of the Wright R-3350
- R-3350-13: 2,200 hp (1,641 kW)
- R-3350-23: 2,200 hp (1,641 kW)
- R-3350-24W: 2,500 hp (1,900 kW)
- R-3350-32W: 3,700 hp (2,800 kW) at 2,400 rpm

- R-3350-53: 2,700 hp (2,013 kW)
- R-3350-85: 2,500 hp (1,900 kW)
- R-3350-89A: 3,500 hp (2,600 kW)
- R-3350-93W: 3,500 hp (2,600 kW)

**Technical features**

Data referring to the R-3350-32W version

- Manufacturer: Curtiss-Wright Corporation
- Number of cylinders: Twin-cylinder 18-cylinder radial engine
- Cooling: air
- Power supply: direct injection
- Distribution: OHV 2 valves per cylinder
- Compressor: double stage centrifugal and two speeds
- Length: 1.985 mm
- Diameter: 1,413 mm
- Displacement: 54.850 cm3
- Reaming: 155.6 mm
- Stroke: 160.2 mm
- Empty weight: 1.212 kg
- Power: 2,500 hp (1,900 kW) to 2,400
- Petrol: 100-130 octane

## Pratt & Whitney R-4360 engine

The Pratt & Whitney R-4360 Wasp Major was the largest and most powerful aviation radial cylinder engine ever produced in series. This engine represented the apex of the development of piston engine technology, or as they are called alternatives today, before the advent of Jet engines and turboprop engines drastically reduced their adoption in the civil and military aeronautical market.

The engine consisted of 28 cylinders arranged on four seven-cylinder stars each.
Each star was slightly rotated compared to the previous one in order to allow the best flow for the cooling air.
Seen from the side, the arrangement of the cylinders assumed a helical aspect.

For this reason it was also nicknamed "Corncob" (corn cob) because the arrangement of the cylinders reminded the seeds on a panicle. The engine had a six-speed mechanical compressor.

Its displacement was 71.4 liters (4360 cubic inches - hence the company's designation as R-4360). The propellers were rotated at a speed equal to half the speed at which the engine turned to prevent the ends, moving, reach a supersonic speed that would degrade its performance.

The first versions of the engine developed 3,000 hp (2,240 kW) but, in recent versions, this had risen to 4,300 hp (3,200 kW).

Despite the weight of the engine ranging from 1,600 to 1,800 kg, its weight / power ratio was among the highest ever achieved by this type of engine.

Engine production took place between 1944 and 1955 for a total of 18.697 pieces.

The Wasp Major was used on the Boeing B-50 bombers, a post-war development of the Boeing B-29 Superfortress, the Convair B-36 and many other civil and military transport aircraft.

**Technical features**

- Manufacturer: Pratt & Whitney
- Number of cylinders: 28-cylinder quadruple star radial engine
- Cooling: air
- Feeding: Stromberg quadruple body carburetors
- Distribution: 2 valves per cylinder
- Compressor: single-phase mechanical centrifugal and variable speed with General Electric CHM-2 turbocharger
- Length: 2.451 mm
- Diameter: 1,397 mm

- Displacement: 71.490 cm3
- Bore: 146 mm
- Stroke: 152 mm
- Compression ratio: 6.7: 1
- Weight / power ratio: 1.83 kW per kg
- Weight: 1.579-1.755 kg
- Power: 3,000 hp (2,240 kW) - 4,300 hp (3,200 kW)
- Gasoline: 108-135 octane

# Versions

## XB-29

The XB-29 was the first prototype of the B-29 for the US Army Air Corps. The aircraft differed from the original design for several improvements, which included more defensive armament, in terms of size and number of pieces, and the introduction of self-supporting tanks.

Two specimens were ordered in August 1940, to these was added a third aircraft ordered in the following December. A simulacrum for static tests was completed in the spring of 1941. A year later, on September 21, 1942 the first flight.

The testing phase continued until February 18, 1943, when the second prototype crashed. At the controls Edmund T. Allen, chief test and head of the Research section of Boeing. After a two-hour flight to test the performance of the propulsion system one of the four engines caught fire; probably due to the significant use of magnesium the fire spread from the engine along the wing frame, causing it to break.

The incident cost the lives of several staff members of the company involved in the design.

After the incident, a joint commission was launched by the US Army Air Force and the United States Congress to investigate the B-29 program. Head Senator Harry S. Truman. The latter wrote a caustic report to encourage the continuation of the program. In the next few months the engines gave several problems in flight tests; for 23 flight tests, 16 engines needed, with a total of only 27 hours of flight. The standard crew was 12 men including the pilot, co-pilot, bomber, navigator, flight engineer, radio operator, radar operator, and five machine-gunners. The first seven

subjects occupied the front of the pressurized cabin, four machine-guns were in the back of the cabin, and the poor tail gunner was "stowed" for the duration of the flight in its small pressurized compartment.
Specimens produced: 3.

## YB-29

The YB-29 was an improved version of the XB-29 to test its use. The testing and evaluation phase began in the summer of 1943, and dozens of aircraft modifications were made during this phase.
The engines were updated by the Wright R-3350-13 to the Wright R-3350-21, in addition four-blade propellers were used, rather than three-blade like in the XB-29.
Various control systems for ranged weapons were tested, in particular the fourth type tested. After evaluating different combinations for the defensive armament, this was eventually standardized with 5 12.7 mm machine guns in pairs mounted towers.
The YB-29 also adopted a better fire control system. Since mid-1943, the Wichita plant began delivering the first fourteen YB-29 aircraft for testing at the 58th Bomb Wing. In YB-29, Sperry turrets were replaced with non-retractable GE-type models, driven by computerized pointers. The GE turrets could be inserted into the artillery piece, but the need for electric current forced the designers to weigh down the aircraft.
Specimens produced: 14.

## B-29

The B-29 was the first serial version of the Superfortress.
Given the urgency with which the new bomber was to be put into service, mass production was started in parallel with the tests to test its use.

For this reason the first series B-29 was completed only two months after the delivery of the first YB-29 of pre-series.

Specimens produced 2.513:

- 1,620 from Boeing-Wichita.
- 536 from Martin-Omaha.
- 357 from the Bell-Marietta.

Variants:

- RB-29: photographic reconnaissance version of the B-29, originally designated as F-13.
- Washington Mk 1: British designation of the 88 B-29 delivered to the Royal Air Force.

Powered by four 2,200 hp Wright R-3350-23 radial engines driving the 7-inch four-bladed propellers, the B-29 could travel 550 km / h to 9,200 meters in height. On long distances the cruising speed was 354 km / h at 7,600 meters.

In September 1943, the first B-29 came out of the Wichita assembly lines, followed by deliveries produced in the following months by the other plants. Some of the last B-29s had a camouflaged livery; the rest were delivered in natural metal color.

The thirty petrol tanks that the airplanes were equipped with, positioned in the wings and in the holds of the bombs, could contain more than 35,000 liters of gasoline. Radar systems have strongly helped flying fortresses both in navigation and in acquiring targets to be bombed.

Like most of the other bombers, the B-29 developed above all in the increase of the defensive firepower, in particular against the frontal attacks of the opposing fighters.

In the case of the B-29, the "dorsal" defense machine guns were increased from two to four. However, the original 20 mm cannon placed in the tail was removed, due to the lines of trajectory so different and difficult to interpret compared to those traced by the beloved 50-caliber machine gun.

The last B-29 was produced by Boeings at the Wichita plant in October 1945.

## B-29A

The B-29A was an improved version of the series B-29.

It was produced exclusively at the Boeing plant in Renton, Washington, first used by the US Navy.

The innovations introduced with the B-29A included an improved wing design and modifications to the defensive armament.

Following the demonstrated weakness of the aircraft in frontal attacks, the number of machine guns in the forward-facing dorsal towers was doubled to four.

The wings of the previous models were built using the sub-assembly of two sections, from the B-29A onwards it began to use a decomposed wing in three sections.

This modification made the assembly of the aircraft easier and led to a stronger chassis. The B-29A remained in production until May 1946, when the last model was completed.

It was widely used during the Korean War, but was soon removed from service with the introduction of jet propelled bombers.

Exemplary products: 1.119.

variants:

- RB-29A: photographic reconnaissance version of the B-29A, originally designated as F-13.

## B-29B

The B-29B was a modified version with 7-8 crewmembers to perform low-altitude raids with incendiary bombs on the Japanese homeland. Since the opposition of the fighters was very small with the advance of the year 1944, many of the USAAF commanders, advanced the proposal that a lighter but faster bomber could have evaded more easily from the Japanese anti-aircraft.

Among the supporters of this line is Curtis LeMay, commander of the 21st Bomber Command.

This variant was then launched to mass production, in which all the defensive armament had been removed, with the sole exception of the caudal turret, in which the M2 cannon was replaced with a pair of 12.7 mm M2 machine guns.

The weight saved allowed to bring the maximum speed of the aircraft from 574 km / h to 586 km / h. All B-29Bs were manufactured by the Bell plant in Marietta, Georgia.

Specimens produced: 311.

## B-29C

The B-29C was a variant of the proposed B-29A, but never realized. It was basically a B-29A re-engineered with a new improved version of the Wright R-3350 engines.

The USAAF originally ordered 5,000 copies, but the request was canceled with the end of the war.

Specimens produced: None.

## B-29D

The B-29D was an improved version of the entire original B-29 design. Introducing new Pratt & Whitney R-4360-35 engines of 3,500 Hp (2,600 kW) each, almost 60% more than the Wright R-3350s of the B-29 series. It presented a new elongated drift and a further reinforced wing. The project was initially named XB-44, then assumed the designation of B-29D

The drastic defense cuts followed at the end of the Second World War reduced the prospects for further development of the B-29 program. Among other things, congress members were reluctant to continue to subsidize projects developed during the conflict. For this reason the B-29D project was redesigned B-50, to make it appear completely renewed also in the name.

The B-29D / B-50 program was then placed, but no B-50s were completed with the old designation of B-29D.

**EB-29**

The designation of EB-29 was used generically to refer to those B-29 modified as mother planes in different experimental programs. The E stands for Exempt, exempt.

- EB-29B: sample number 44-84111 modified in the bombiero compartment to test the launch and recovery operations of the McDonnell XF-85 Goblin parasitic fighter, destined to be boarded on the Convair B-36.
- ETB-29A: a TB-29A (serial number 44-62093) modified as part of the Tom-Tom Project for flying in the wingtips of a pair of Republic F-84D Thunderjet as a parasitic fighter.
- ETB-29A and the two F-84s were destroyed in an accident on 24 April 1953.
- EGB-29: aircraft modified in the bomber compartment to transport the Bell X-1 in flight, a supersonic research aircraft that was not able to take off autonomously. Intended for a similar task for the next Bell X-2, it was replaced by a Boeing B-50.

## SB-29

The SB-29 "Super Dumbo" was the designation of the B-29 adopted for SAR (Search And Rescue) tasks, search and rescue, in the post-war period. The bomber was modified to carry a parachute A-3 lifeboat under the fuselage. The SB-29 found employment as a means of rescue for the crews of airplanes engaged on a wide-ranging mission on the water.

All the defensive armament was maintained with the sole exception of the lower turret towards the stern.

It was also used during the Korean War in the mid-fifties.

The nickname came from 'Dumbo', the nickname given by the crews of B-29 forced emergency ditches to lifeboats.

Converted specimens: 16.

## TB-29

TB-29 was the designation of the B-29 converted to training tasks for the bomber crews. Some of these were also used for towing targets, and the TB-29 designation was also used for aircraft used only for this purpose.

Probably the most significant role they had in the fifties, when they were used as "radar targets" to fine-tune the new USAF fighter interception tactics.

## WB-29

WB-29 was the designation of the B-29 converted for weather missions (the letter W in the abbreviation of Weather, time). These aircraft typically carried out standard data collection missions, but flights to the eye of a hurricane or typhoon for information gathering were also made. Another peculiar task they were involved in was the collection of air samples to measure radioactivity levels following nuclear tests. In mid-1951, three B-29s were modified to participate in the Airborne Early Warning program, which would lead to the construction of the first AWACS. The upper section of the front of the fuselage underwent extensive modifications to accommodate an AN / APS-20C research radar.

The interior also underwent extensive modifications to accommodate radar and electronic countermeasure systems (ECM).

This led to the development of the first AWACS, including the Lockheed C-121 Warning Star.

Converted specimens: 3.

## XB-39

The XB-39 was a single YB-29 model modified to use the Allison V-3420-17 V engines featuring liquid cooling.

This change was requested by the USAAF in the event that the engines destined for the B-29, the Wright R-3350 could present insurmountable difficulties in the development phase.

General Motors was responsible for converting the prototype. Since the problems in the development of the R-3350 were solved, only one XB-39 was built and no pre-war aircraft were ordered.

Converted specimens: 1.

## Tupolev Tu-4

Soviet copy of the B-29, with some improvements to engines and armament.

During 1945, three Boeing B-29s were forced into emergency landings in the Soviet Union after actions against the Japanese territory.

Since the USSR was not at war with Japan, the crews were interned, only to be released later. For the B-29 the fate was very different.

64

The Soviet Air Force at the time lacked a valid long-range bomber, so it was ordered to OKB Tupolev to study the B-29 to produce it in series in the USSR. The exercise of retro-engineering was successful and the first model flew on May 19, 1947 and production of series was started immediately. Externally identical to the B-29, the Tupolev Tu-4, Bull (Taurus) in the NATO code name differed for the defensive armament.

Another difference was that the project had been re-engineered to agree to a mass production based on the metric decimal system.
The Tu-4 was slightly slower and heavier than the western original.

**Ilyushin Il-9**

Exact copy built under license.

## Test benches

Several B-29s of the different series at the end of their careers were converted to serve as flying test benches. All these aircraft received their own designations, even when it was a single converted specimen. Among these aircraft:

- XB-29E: a converted sample to test electronic shooting control systems.
- B-29F: six units converted for service in Arctic climates in Alaska.
- XB-29G: a private armament B-29B used as a test bench for jet engines. The jet engines to be tested were installed in the bomber compartment; during the flight the engine was exposed to the external air flow and switched on to test its behavior. Among the engines tested: Allison J35, General Electric J47 and General Electric J73.
- XB-29H: test with new defensive armament.
- YB-29J: 6 specimens of B-29 of different series modified to test new engines for the civil market. New R-3350-79 thrusters, new Curtiss propellers and new 'Andy Gump' engine caps were adopted, in which the oil coolers had separate air intakes. Later the six aircraft were subjected to changes:
- YKB-29J: two YB-29J were developed as prototypes of rigid boom type aircrafts (Flying Boom) for refueling in flight.
- RB-29J: the remaining 4 YB-29J were converted into reconnaissance aircraft, also referred to as FB-29J

Numerous B-29 specimens were converted to develop refueling systems in flight at the end of the 1940s:

- KB-29M: flexible probe tankers, 92 units. At first the aircraft did not adopt a British-style flexible probe, but a more complicated system based on a hook.
- B-29MR: aircraft receiving the KB-29M program, 74 copies.
- YKB-29T: modified KB-29M tanker to accommodate a pair of wing-end probes, in order to supply three aircraft at the same time. It served as a prototype for the Boeing B-50KB-50D.
- KB-29P: rigid rod tankers, 116 units. The technique was developed by Boeing to transfer large quantities of fuel more rapidly. The rigid shaft was installed aft of the tank and ended with two wings. The fins allowed the operator on board the aerator to maneuver the probe. This method quickly became widespread, being used on the KB-50, KC-97 Stratotanker. It is still used on the KC-135 Stratotanker and KC-10 Extender.

# Enola Gay

Enola Gay is the B-29 Superfortress bomber, (B-29-45-MO, serial number 44-86292, victor number 82) that on August 6, 1945, shortly before the end of the Second World War, launched on the Japanese city of Hiroshima is the first atomic bomb in history to have been used in war, nicknamed Little Boy.

Because of its role in the atomic bombings of Hiroshima and Nagasaki, its name has been synonymous with the controversy over the bombings themselves.

- Enola Gay was the name of the pilot's mother, Paul Tibbets.

In 1994, the plane gained more national attention in the United States when a Smithsonian Institution exhibit at the National Air and Space Museum in Washington was changed due to a dispute over the historical content of the exhibition.

Since 2003, Enola Gay has been exhibiting at the Steven F. Udvar-Hazy Center at Dulles International Airport, Virginia. The Enola Gay (B-29-45-MO, serial number 44-86292, victor number 82) was assigned to the 393th bomber squadron, 509th Composite Group of the USAF, and flew the mission of August 6 starting from Tinian, a large island with several USAF air bases in the archipelago of the Mariana Islands.

The plane was one of fifteen B-29s with the latest modification "Silverplate", necessary to release atomic bombs.

The Enola Gay was built by Glenn L. Martin Company in the Omaha, Nebraska plant, in what is now the Offutt Air Force Base, and personally selected by Colonel Paul Tibbets, commander of the 509th Composite Group on

May 9, 1945, when he was still on the assembly line, like the B-29 that would have used for the mission of the release of the first atomic bomb.

The Enola Gay at the Steven F. Udvar-Hazy Center

The plane was accepted by the United States Army Air Forces (USAAF) on May 18, 1945 and assigned to the crew B-9 (captain Robert Lewis, commander of the plane), who flew the plane from Omaha to the base of the 509th at the Wendover Army Air Field, Utah, June 14, 1945. Thirteen days later he left Wendover for Guam, where the bombs were modified, and continued for Tinian on July 6th. He was assigned victor number 12, which was later changed to 82.

After completing eight training and two combat missions in July, the plane was used on July 31 in a test of the actual mission, with a fake "Little Boy" that was dropped off Tinian.

On August 5, 1945, during the preparations for the first atomic mission, Tibbets gave the plane the name of his mother, Enola Gay Tibbets (1893-1983, who bore that name from a heroine of a novel).

According to Gordon Thomas and Max Morgan-Witts, the regularly assigned commander of the plane, Robert Lewis, was unhappy to be bypassed by Tibbets for this important mission, and was furious when he arrived in front of the plane on the morning of 6 August and saw him painted with the new name.

Tibbets himself, interviewed by Tinian at the end of that day by a war correspondent, confessed to feeling a little embarrassed at having associated his mother's name with such a fateful mission.

Together with Enola Gay, another six planes participated in the mission; three meteorological reconnaissance aircraft, at the head of the flight group: Straight Flush, commanded by Claude Eatherly, en route to Hiroshima, Jabbitt III, led by John Wilson, en route to Kokura and Full House, piloted by Ralph Taylor, in flight towards Nagasaki.

The seven B-29s of the Hiroshima Mission were:
- Enola Gay, piloted by Col. Tibbets carrying the Little Boy uranium bomb.

70

- The Great Artiste, piloted by Maj. Charles Sweeney, who carried the three instruments used to measure the effects of the atomic explosion.
- # 91 (then nameless - Necessary Evil later), led by Capt. George Marquardt, who transported scientific observers.
- The Top Secret, with Capt. Chuck Knight in the driver's seat, was the reserve aircraft and flew to Iwo Jima in the event of mechanical problems with Enola Gay.
- Straight Flush acting as a meteorological reconnaissance aircraft and flying towards the main Hiroshima target.
- Jabbitt III in charge of the meteorological survey of the Kokura secondary target.
- The Full House with meteorological recognition function of the alternative Nagasaki target.

The main focus was Hiroshima, but if bad weather prevented the bombing, Kokura and Nagasaki were the potential alternative targets. Charles Sweeney's Great Artiste and George Marquart's anonymous aircraft No. 91, later named Necessary Evil, carrying equipment for filming and other special equipment, were escorted by Enola Gay. The seventh aircraft in order of takeoff was the Top Secret driven by Chuck McKnight, with the task of flying to Iwo Jima while remaining available in case of need. That evening, after the meal, the seven crews taking part in the mission gathered for a brief pre-flight briefing. Later, at 11 pm, the crews of the Enola Gay and the other two planes that would accompany him to his goal received the final briefing; that was the first time they discussed the power of the bomb they would have dropped. They were stunned, the magnitude of the explosion required rapid evasive maneuvers to be carried out immediately after the bomb was released, procedures to which they had been trained in a precise manner.

Tibbets chose:

- Theodore "Dutch" Van Kirk as his navigator.
- Thomas W. Ferebee as a bomber. Both had participated with Tibbets in the bombing missions in Europe during the first years of the war.

The other crew members of the Enola Gay were:

- Robert A. Lewis, co-pilot.
- Wyatt E. Duzenbury, flight engineer.
- George R. "Bob" Caron, tail shooter.
- Joseph A. Stiborik, radar operator.
- Richard H. "Junior" Nelson, radio operator.
- Robert Shumard, assistant engineer of the flight.
- Jacob Beser, "Raven" official radar operator.
- Navy Captain William S. "Deak" Parsons, an arms officer borrowed from the Manhattan Project, who had led to the construction of the bomb.
- His assistant, Morris R. Jeppson, specialist in the proximity quill system.

The names of all members, excluding the last three, whose functions were largely linked to the bomb, would later be etched on the side of the plane to remember their participation in the historic flight.

The mission on Hiroshima was described as impeccable from the tactical point of view, and Enola Gay returned without inconvenience to his Tinian base.

The take-off took place as scheduled at 02.45. Tibbets takes the plane at low altitude while Captain Parsons went into the back to arm the bomb. When they reached Iwo Jima, Tibbets circled the island to await the arrival of the other two planes, then together gradually resume altitude. They still had 1,700 miles to travel to Hiroshima and the crew took turns to rest. This would have been the thirteenth longest mission, and for a while there was little to do. Claude Eatherly, on board the plane that preceded them, reached Hiroshima, found the sky clean, and communicated by radio. Then he turned back to the base: Hiroshima had become the target.

As the Gay Enola approached the city, the crew was able to see it clearly from over fifty miles. Van Kirk called Ferebee and made a long course for the bombing, probably eight or nine minutes, possibly adjusting his aim on the target, the Aioi bridge characterized by the shape of a T. He remembers: "If we had ever carried out a bombing route like this in Europe and for such a long time, they would certainly have thrown us down, but there was no opposition ".

As soon as the bomb dropped, the plane reared, lightened its weight, and Tibbets made a tight turn. Forty three seconds later, when the bomb reached the detonation altitude of 570 meters above the ground, the sky lit up. Even if they were wearing dark glasses, the crew felt like someone had lit a flash in their eyes. The shock wave arrived after another forty-five seconds. This was the moment of truth. The plane stumbled, but resisted the explosion. The most imminent danger had passed. Meanwhile, the atomic mushroom rose rapidly, something that had never been seen before, reaching an altitude of sixteen kilometers, five kilometers higher than their flight altitude. Nelson recalls: "The city was just an immense confusion of flames and dust".

Van Kirk says, "It looked like a vessel where it was boiling tar." There was not much to understand, so the three planes returned to the base. Nelson recalls that during the return journey they said: "that the war was over .... We can not think how they can go on yet .... with this device". Looking over his shoulder, Ferebee said, "We do not think we're rewarded with either our aircraft or our own plane ...

just to show what he did at that time, things are very different today, and people see things very differently. But we must take into account the period in which the facts occurred ".

About an hour before the bombing, the Japanese radar network launched an immediate alarm, detecting the approach of a large number of American aircraft headed to the southern part of Japan. The alarm was also spread through radio broadcasts in many cities in Japan, including Hiroshima.

The planes approached the shores of the Japanese archipelago at a very high height. Shortly before 8:00 am, the Hiroshima radar station determined that the number of aircraft entering the Japanese airspace was low, probably no more than three, so the air alarm was resized (the Japanese military command, in fact, had decided, to save fuel, not to fly their airplanes for small American airborne formations).

The Hiroshima mission did not end the war. Despite the scale of the destruction, the Japanese did not surrender immediately. Nelson thought: "Something else was needed, and that something was the second bomb ... The second bomb was a necessity .... It was supposed to prove that you had more than one weapon." He felt that the bomb dropped on Nagasaki would cause surrender within three days. In fact, the first atomic bombing was followed three days later by that of another B-29 (BOCKSCAR), piloted by Major Charles W. Sweeney, who dropped a second nuclear bomb called "Fat Man" on Nagasaki. The Nagasaki mission, on the other hand, has been described as tactically incorrect; even if he achieved his goals, he went through several execution errors and Bockscar barely had the fuel needed for an emergency landing in Okinawa. The 4.2-ton bomb, called 'Little Boy', was released at 8.15. Exploding into the air just before touching Hiroshima soil, the bomb developed a heat wave that reached 4,000 degrees Celsius in a radius of more than 4 kilometers, followed by a sinister smoke mushroom. One hundred and forty thousand of the 350,000 inhabitants of the city died instantly, but the atomic explosion left a sinister trail of death and suffering for years on the city. In the end, in Hiroshima, the ascertained victims of the atomic bomb were 221,823, with those who lost their lives due to the damage caused by nuclear radiation.

On November 6, 1945, Lewis reported the Enola Gay to the United States, landing on the new base of the 509th Roswell Army Air Field, New Mexico, on November 8th.

On 29 April 1946, Enola Gay abandoned Roswell as part of Operation Crossroads and flew to Kwajalein on 1 May. He was not chosen to take the Bikini Atoll test and left Kwajalein on July 1, the day of the test, and reached the Fairfield-Suisun Army Air Field, California the following day.

The decision was made to preserve the plane and on July 24, 1946 it was moved to the Davis-Monthan Air Force Base, Arizona, in order to prepare it for the deposit.

On 30 August the ownership of the aircraft was transferred to the Smithsonian Institution and was removed from the USAAF inventory; since then it has been temporarily stored in a series of positions:

- 1 September 1946, Davis-Monthan AFB.
- July 3, 1949, Orchard Place Air Field, Park Ridge, Illinois, flown here by General Tibbets for acceptance by the Smithsonian.
- 12 January 1952, Pyote Air Force Base, Texas, moved after O'Hare's position was confirmed.
- 2 December 1953, Andrews Air Force Base, Maryland.
- 10 August 1960, the disassembly at Andrews was initiated by Smithsonian personnel.

- July 21, 1961, the components were transported to the Smithsonian Depot Center in Suitland, Maryland.

The renovation began on December 5, 1984, permanently at the "Paul E. Garber" Preservation, Restructuring and Storage Center in Suitland.

Enola Gay found itself at the center of a controversy at the Smithsonian Institution in 1994, when the museum showed off its fuselage as part of the exhibit commemorating the fiftieth anniversary of the atomic bombing of Hiroshima. The exhibition "The Crossroads: The End of World War II, the Atomic Bomb, and the Cold War" was prepared by the Smithsonian National Air and Space Museum and staged around a restored version of the Gay Island.

Critics, particularly the American Legion and the Air Force Association, accused the show of focusing too much on bomb victims, rather than on the reasons that led to the bombing or discussion of the role it played in ending the war. The exhibition brought to the national attention many lasting academic and political issues, linked to retrospective views of the bombing, and in the end, after attempts to review the exhibition in order to satisfy the various groups in competition, the same was canceled on January 30th. 1995, although the fuselage still went on show.

On 18 May 1998 the fuselage was returned to the Garber Facility for the final restoration. Since then the entire plane has been restored for static exhibits and is currently one of the main pieces on display at the National Air and Space Museum near Dulles International Airport. As a consequence of the controversy mentioned above, the information panels around the aircraft only report the same brief technical data common to the other aircraft in the museum, without discussing the controversial issues. The plane is protected by various means to prevent a repetition of the vandalisms that were attempted against it the first time it was put on display. The four aluminum propellers, which were used during the bombing mission to save weight, ended up at Texas A & M University.

One of these, reduced to 3 meters, provides the boost to the Oran W. Nicks low-speed wind tunnel.

A 1,250 kVA electric motor provides a constant rotation (900 RPM) and the inclination of the propeller blades (pitch) is varied to control the wind speed (up to 320 kilometers per hour) in the tunnel.

The crew of the Enola Gay in the mission of 6 August 1945 was composed of twelve people:

- Colonel Paul Tibbets, pilot. In 1959 Tibbets was promoted to the rank of general brigadier, then retired from the US Air Force on August 31, 1966. A few years before his death he declared in an interview: "I'm not proud of killing 80,000 people, but I'm proud to have left from nothing, having organized the whole operation and having performed the job perfectly, the night I sleep well ". He died in Columbus on 1 November 2007 at the age of 92; fearing of possible retaliation and protests, because over the years he had been repeatedly threatened with vandalism on his burial, by his will Tibbets asked to be cremated and, in fact, his ashes were scattered on the English Channel that had flown over times during the war.

- Captain Robert A. Lewis, co-pilot. It was Captain Robert Lewis, after checking with binoculars the effects of the bomb dropped on Hiroshima, writing in his diary: "My God what have we done?".

- Major Thomas Ferebee, bomber. Thomas Wilson Ferebee, the man who dropped the atomic bomb on Hiroshima, died March 17, 2000 at the age of 81. He left his wife, Mary Ann, and four children. "I never felt guilty," he said in one of his last interviews, "but I regret that many people died of the bomb and I hate to think that something like this must have happened to end the war." Ferebee had the rank of major and was a veteran of the war in Europe and the Pacific when on August 6, 1945, he dropped the bomb that killed 100,000 people in Hiroshima. Ferebee had a long experience of raids on enemy territory, purchased in 1942 on France occupied by the Nazis. He had been the head bomber of the first air strike launched by allies in Europe in the light of day. Become a man in wartime, he participated in the front line of all the military vicissitudes of the United States. Before retirement he fought in Korea and Vietnam. Besides him, only another man had dropped an atomic bomb in a war action, Kermit Beahanan, the bomber that destroyed Nagasaki on 9 August 1945, died in 1989. In 1995, while his flight companions celebrated with bold declarations the fiftieth anniversary of the bomb that gave the victory to the United States, Ferebee had taken a more moderate attitude. "We have to look back, he said, and remember what a single bomb could do. And we must realize that this can never happen again ".

- Captain Theodore Van Kirk, navigator on board the Enola Gay, who admitted: "I left Hiroshima, but Hiroshima never left me". He first identified the unmistakable "T" shaped bridge, the target of reference, next to the dome of the building of the Industrial Exposition.

- Lieutenant Jacob Beser, radar specialist; the only one to fly also in the bombing of Nagasaki.

- Captain William Sterling "Deak" Parsons, responsible for armaments. To avoid the possibility of a nuclear explosion if the plane had crashed or burned during take-off, he decided to arm the bomb in flight.

- Second Lieutenant Morris R. Jeppson, assistant to the Armament Manager. Jeppson and Captain William Parsons were tasked with arming the bomb during the flight from the island of Tinian to Japan before they reached Hiroshima and removed the quills from the bomb, just before it was dropped. The bomb during the flight was protected from an accidental explosion by four cigarette-sized safety plugs, about three centimeters in length, inserted into the internal electrical system because no voltage fluctuation triggered the mechanism. Jeppson had kept two of these and were sold to retired physicist Clay Perkins for $ 167,000, believed by the latter to be the most important objects of the last century because they were components of the first nuclear device in history. In the 1950s, Jeppson worked as a researcher at Lawrence Livermore National Laboratory in California, helping to develop far more powerful and devastating atomic nuclear weapons. Other major technological innovations that have helped to develop are: microwave technology and stabilizers mounted on helicopters.

- Sergeant Joe S. Stiborik, radar. Curiosity: his wife Helen still keeps a bunch of keys from the Gay Island.

- Technical sergeant Robert Caron, tail machine-gunner, the only defender of the twelve members of the B-29 Enola Gay crew. Caron was also the only photographer on board who took photographs when the atomic mushroom went up.

- Sergeant Robert Shumard, assistant flight engineer.

- Private First Class Richard Nelson, radio operator.

- Technical Sergeant Wyatt Duzenberry, flight engineer.

Tibbets left the US Air Force in 1966 with the rank of General and set up a taxi-jet company in Ohio. He died on 1 November 2007 at the age of 92.

According to the family friend Gerry Newhouse, he said he did not celebrate a funeral and did not put a headstone on his grave, for fear that it would become a place for protest demonstrations.

In an interview in December 2003, Tibbets states that he did not declare the mission to the crew until they were en route. The flight crew, technicians, engineers, suppliers and other support people did not know the purpose of the mission or the final result of their task. He went to the back of the plane to give the crew the details about the weapon they called "gimmick". "Today we are about to launch a special weapon on the target, which is Hiroshima," Tibbets said to the crew.

"The explosion and the air movement will be like hell, you do not imagine what you are about to see." Tibbets explains that the reason he revealed the secret before the bomb was released was to acquaint his crew with the severity of their work that day. Tibbets also confirmed that he offered cyanide to the crew members in case something went wrong. Only two accepted it. The autograph copy of one of the Enola Gay logbooks was awarded at an auction in New York for $ 50,000 (April 2015). This was announced by the Bonhams auction house. Robert Lewis, co-pilot of the flying super fortitude B-29 had made this copy in 1945 at the request of a New York Times journalist. The original was written on August 6, 1945, flying to Hiroshima, and he described the mission that was classified as top secret.

He had entitled the document "Letter for Mom and Dad", since it was forbidden to reveal the details of the mission, the auction house explained.

"I am convinced that the whole crew felt that this experience represented more than any human being could have imagined" wrote Robert Lewis.

The original had instead been auctioned for $ 391,000 in 2002 from the Christies auction house.

# Little Boy

Little Boy was the code name of the Mk.1 bomb, the second atomic bomb built under the Manhattan Project (code name of the research program conducted by the United States during the Second World War, which led to the construction of the first atomic bombs ) and the first nuclear weapon in history to have been used in a conflict through the bombing of Hiroshima during the last days of the Second World War. To make this bomb uranium oxides of different quality and origin were used.

Most of it was enriched in the facilities of the Oak Ridge National Laboratory in Tennessee, mainly through the gas diffusion method of uranium hexafluoride, marginally with other techniques. The Mk.1 was equipped with a shell of conventional steel form, 3 meters long and with a diameter of 0.71 meters, and weighed 4.037 kilograms.

It was a "gun type" atomic bomb with fissile material consisting of highly enriched uranium. In the case of "Little Boy", the "bullet" of enriched uranium was weighing 38.53 kilograms and the target, likewise enriched uranium, weighed 25.6 kilograms.

The bomb contained a total of 64.13 kilograms of 80% enriched uranium, equal to 2.4 critical masses. The projectile consisted of a hollow cylinder consisting of nine washers, while the target was a cylinder composed of six washers with an internal diameter of 25.4 mm, that is the one needed to contain a steel bar of the same diameter that would have constituted the "backbone" of the super-critical mass. The target was completed on July 24, 1945 where the washers that would make up the projectile were merged between June 15, 1945 and July 3 of the same year. The barrel was a regular, 183 cm long, modified anti-aircraft gun, with an external diameter of 165 mm and a caliber of 76 mm and able to withstand a pressure of 2,700 Bar.

"Little Boy", the first atomic bomb to have operational use.

The barrels were tested by firing each of two or three rounds with 90 kilogram bullets at a speed of 300 meters per second.

It had been calculated that the fissile activity of the critical mass of "Little Boy" lasted a total of 1.35 milliseconds and that the first part of which (of a duration equal to 0.5 milliseconds) occurred during the approach of the projectile to the target ( and therefore even before the union of the two sub-critical masses). In case of failure to start the chain reaction, some "ABNER" initiators in beryllium-polonium alloy would act as a source of neutrons capable of externally triggering the reaction.

The decision to add the "ABNER" to the trigger mechanism was taken by Robert Oppenheimer only on March 15, 1945.

As a result of this, sixteen of these initiators were sent directly to the US military base of the island of Tinian

(Marianne archipelago) in the Pacific Ocean, where the final assembly of the bomb was being carried out, and four of them were assembled for the first time in it.

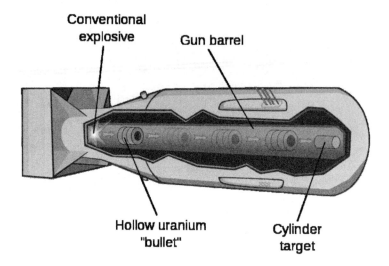

Conventional explosive

Gun barrel

Hollow uranium "bullet"

Cylinder target

The members of "Little Boy" were sent to the island of Tinian from the month of May 1945, ie even before the "Trinity test" was carried out.

The Indianapolis cruiser, starting on July 16, 1945 from San Francisco and arriving on the island ten days later, transported the parts to make up the body of the bomb and the bullet while three C-54 planes brought the target on July 28, 1945. The bomb (named "L11") was set up on July 31, 1945. Its use was originally planned first for August 1, 1945 and later for August 3, 1945 but the bad weather conditions prevented the bomber's take-off in those days.

On 4 August 1945 it was then decided to take off two days later, and the following day the bomb was loaded in the hold of the heavy strategic bomber Boeing B-29-45-MO Superfortress of the United States Army Air Forces (serial number 44-86292) renamed with the pseudonym of "Enola

Gay". The release of the Mk.1 "Little Boy" bomb on the center of the Japanese city of Hiroshima took place at 8:15:17 local time (JST) on 6 August 1945 at an altitude of 9,467 meters and the bomb exploded at a predetermined height of 580 meters as calculated by John von Neumann to have the greatest destructive effects.

The person in charge pointing, Colonel Thomas Wilson Ferebee, had targeted the "T" Aioi bridge over the Ota River, which was missed for less than 250 meters, through the Norden bomber pointing device.

The energy released in the explosion was initially calculated between 12.5 and 18 kilotons (ie between 52 and 66 TJ).

Nevertheless, for several years there was never a precise estimate and the estimated power was indicated from 12.5 to 20 kilotons.

A more detailed study conducted in 2002 found that, realistically, the power developed was about 16 kilotons, ie 63 TJ, and that therefore only 0.7 kilograms of the 64.13 kilograms of enriched uranium contained in the bomb (equal to 1, 1%) suffered fission in the explosion.

In Hiroshima, between 66,000 and 78,000 people died instantly from the nuclear explosion, and a similar figure was injured. A large number of people died in the months and years after due to radiation and many pregnant women lost their children or gave birth to deformed children.

The detonation of "Little Boy" was the first nuclear explosion of the history based on uranium (the "Trinity test" had in fact made use of a weapon to plutonium).

The "Little Boy" bomb was therefore an unproven prototype and, in fact, its launch on Hiroshima therefore represented a real test of operation.

Previous experiments of controlled uranium fission had allowed scientists to pack a weapon without the need to perform a real test before being used in the field.

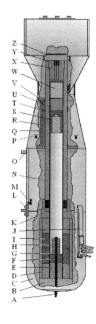

Cross-section drawing of Y-1852 Little Boy showing major mechanical component placement. Drawing is shown to scale. Numbers in ( ) indicate quantity of identical components. Not shown are the APS-13 radar units, clock box with pullout wires, baro switches and tubing, batteries, and electrical wiring. (John Coster-Mullen)

Z) Armor Plate
Y) Mark XV electric gun primers (3)
X) Gun breech with removable inner plug
W) Cordite powder bags (4)
V) Gun tube reinforcing sleeve
U) Projectile steel back
T) Projectile Tungsten-Carbide disk
S) U-235 projectile rings (9)
R) Alignment rod (3)
Q) Armored tube containing primer wiring (3)
P) Baro ports (8)
O) Electrical plugs (3)
N) 6.5" bore gun tube
M) Safing/arming plugs (3)
L) Lift lug
K) Target case gun tube adapter
J) Yagi antenna assembly (4)
I) Four-section 13" diameter Tungsten-Carbide tamper cylinder sleeve
H) U-235 target rings (6)
G) Polonium-Beryllium initiators (4)
F) Tungsten-Carbide tamper plug
E) Impact absorbing anvil
D) K-46 steel target liner sleeve
C) Target case forging
B) 15" diameter steel nose plug forging
A) Front nose locknut attached to 1" diameter main steel rod holding target components

Moreover, the United States of America did not have enough before the end of the second world war of enriched uranium to make an experimental uranium bomb before the use of "Little Boy". Finally, nuclear material was very expensive and so it was preferred not to use it for testing.

Although the design of "Little Boy" was occasionally used in other experimental projects, in essence his project based on the ballistic detonation system, although it was conceptually very simple to develop, was abandoned almost immediately because, for reasons of character technically, it is less efficient than implosion and is also less secure.

An accidental rupture of the bomb, the acceleration produced by the involuntary uncoupling before the time or its fall in water could in fact release lethal doses of radiations or, in extreme cases, also produce an involuntary detonation.

# Bockscar

Bockscar (or even Bock's Car or Bocks Car) is the B-29 Superfortress bomber (sample number 44-27297) which dropped "Fat Man", the name given to the second atomic bomb that hit the city of Nagasaki, Japan, on 9 August 1945. This second launch marked the end of the Second World War.

On the day of the launch the crew was not the usual one but another B-29, the "The Great Artiste", and in command was Major Charles W. Sweeney of Massachusetts. The primary goal was Kokura, but that day the sky was obscured by clouds; since the commander had the order to disengage in conditions of maximum visibility, he had to proceed towards the secondary objective, Nagasaki. There, too, the sky was cloudy, but since the fuel was rapidly diminishing and Major Sweeney did not want to abandon the bomb at sea, it was decided to proceed with a radar bombardment.

There was, however, an opening large enough in the clouds to allow identification to view the city: the bomb was launched 3/4 miles from the planned point and exploded at about 500 meters in height. This caused a relatively lower number of victims (40,000 people) than the first bombing, because the explosion was contained by the Urakami valley. The B-29 did not have enough fuel to return to the base of Tinian or Iwo Jima and the commander was forced to make an emergency landing on the island of Okinawa, practically without fuel. Before the Bockscar another B-29, the Enola Gay, had dropped the first nuclear bomb in the history of the city of Hiroshima. According to the United States Army Air Forces (USAAF), the destruction of the two cities should have made the Japanese understand the American will and ability to conduct these attacks as long as they wanted.

Many believe that the two atomic bombings gave a great impulse to the Japanese surrender, definitively ending the Second World War.

Dayton, Ohio - Boeing B-29 "Bockscar" Superfortress at the National Museum of the United States Air Force.

Others argue that the Japanese were already organizing the surrender, asking the Soviet Union to intervene as a mediator, and that the two bombings, absolutely inhumane and immoral as the cause of the death of hundreds of thousands of civilians, had the only result of accelerating the surrender. Sometimes we refer to this aircraft as "Bocks Car" or "Bock's Car": the name painted on the nose after the mission does not have an apostrophe and is all in capital letters. The name was given by the regular crew pilot, Frederick C. Bock.

Initially there was confusion about the name of the plane because initially the press declared that the second bomb was dropped by the Great Artiste; in fact, it had to be this second plane to release it, but when it became clear that there was not enough time to transfer the equipment from the Great Artiste to the Bockscar, the crews were exchanged. The Bocks Car was withdrawn from service in September 1946 and was semi-abandoned near Tucson, Arizona. It remained until September 1961, when it was transported and exhibited at the National Museum of the United States Air Force at the Wright-Patterson air base near Dayton (Ohio). Near the plane, a sign reads: "The aircraft that ended WWII" ("The plane that ended the Second World War").

Crew of the "Fat Man" mission

- Major Charles W. Sweeney, pilot.
- Captain James Van Pelt, navigator.
- Capt. Raymond "Kermit" Beahan, in charge of the bombing.
- Lieutenant Charles Donald Albury, co-pilot.
- Lieutenant Fred Olivi, co-pilot.
- Corporal Abe Spitzer, radio operator.
- Sergeant Major John D. Kuharek, on board engineer.
- Sgt. Ray Gallagher, machine-gunner, on-board engineer assistant.
- Sgt. Edward Buckley, radar operator.
- Sgt. Albert Dehart, tail machine-gunner.

Navy personnel were also on board:

- Cmdr Frederick L. Ashworth, bomb attendant.
- Lt. Philip Barnes, assistant to the admiral.
- Lt. Jacob Beser, radio countermeasure officer.

**Fat Man**

Fat Man (in Italian "ciccione", a name that is also used to indicate generically even the first bombs based on the same project) was the criptonimo of the bomb Model 1561 (Mk.2), the third atomic bomb prepared as part of the Project Manhattan that, like "Little Boy", also found a military application, as the second and last nuclear device ever used in combat, with the raid on Nagasaki, at the end of the Second World War.

Full-scale reproduction of the bomb called "Fat Man".

The Model 1561 Mk.2 was 2.34 meters long, with a diameter of 1.52 meters, weighed 4,545 kilograms.
From a constructive point of view, it was a bomb similar to "The Gadget".
The 140 cm diameter sphere framed in dural was enclosed in an aerodynamic shape outer shell in the shape of a watermelon to which were added additional components necessary for loading, transport, armament and use of the

bomb on the theater of battle, such as safety fuses, radar system, hinges, aluminum stabilizing tail, barometer, clocks, antenna.

Bomb scheme:
1. Fast explosive.
2. Slow explosive.
3. Tamper/Pusher.
4. Neutron initiator.
5. Plutonium core.
6. Spherical shockwave compresses core.

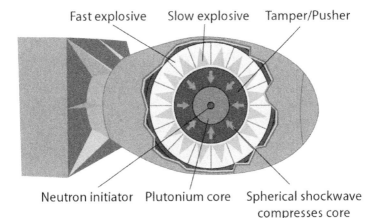

List of main components of the bomb:
1. Security fuses.
2. Radar antenna.
3. Battery used by detonators to produce the explosion.
4. X-Unit, unit that manages the detonators.
5. Hinges to move the bomb.
6. Pentagonal explosive (12 units around the nucleus, consisting of both high and low potential explosives).

7. Hexagonal explosive (20 units around the nucleus, consisting of both high and low potential explosives).
8. Aluminum stabilizing tail.
9. Dural casing with a diameter of 140 centimeters.
10. Cones containing the nucleus.
11. Explosive cells (explosive both at high and low potential).
12. Nuclear material (see image of the "Christy Gadget" section for internal details).
13. Plate with instruments (radar barometer and clocks).
14. Barotube manifold.

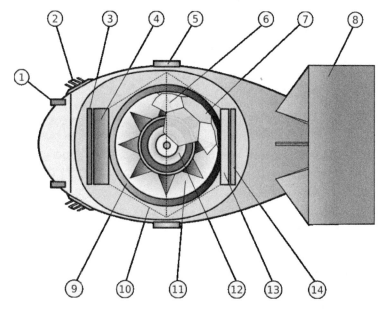

On August 9, 1945 at 11:02 am local time the Model 1561 "Fat Man" bomb was dropped by the B-29 bomber of the United States Army Air Forces named "BOCKSCAR" (of the same department of the "Enola Gay") piloted by Major

Charles Sweeney on the Mitsubishi factory in Nagasaki city in Japan.

The bomb exploded at a height of 550 meters over the city and developed a power of 25 kilotons, a power therefore much higher than the bomb "Little Boy" that exploded three days earlier on Hiroshima but, since Nagasaki was built on a hilly terrain, the number of deaths was lower than those produced by the first bomb.

Between 20,000 and 39,000 people were instantly killed by the nuclear explosion and it is estimated that around 25,000 were injured. Many thousands of people also died later for radiation. The United States of America produced a small number of "Fat Man" bombs (which in its final version, called Mk.3, had a potential of 19-23 kilotons) after the war.

These bombs were, in fact, very delicate and not suitable for long storage.

The project was taken from the "Mk.4 Fat Man" bomb that was similar in principle but designed to be stored for long periods, suitable for use even for non-experts and equipped with a much safer and more efficient detonation system (based on on 60 implosion points compared to 32 of the "Fat Man" bomb).

# The bombing of Akita

On August 14, 1945, from the advanced American base in the Pacific Ocean (island of Guam), they took flight (for the longest transfer of the Second World War 7,800 km round trip) 143 flying super-fortresses of the type B29 belonging to the 315th Group from American bombing. The intent of this long flight was to bomb the oil refineries of the Japanese city of Akita, as these refineries were the last hope for Japan to continue the war. A week after the release of the two Atomic bombs on the cities of Hiroschima and Nagasaki, the Empire of the rising sun still did not show signs of wanting to surrender to the American superpower.

So much so that the President U.S.A. Truman had planned to invade the whole of Japan or to continue to hammer the Japanese cities with Atomic bombs up to a number of seven (as many as had been built by the Americans until that date). Calculating how much an invasion of Japan would cost in human lives, calculating also to which radiation the American soldiers would have been submitted advancing in a scene bombed by numerous Atomic bombs, it was concluded that for the moment a strategic bombardment was enough to destroy the refineries of the city of Akita. On August 14, 1945 at 1:00 pm with the deafening noise of hundreds of star engines, they took flight from the island of Guam 143 flying super fortitudes B29.

At the Japanese headquarters in Tokyo, military conspirators were plotting "against Peace". Major of the Japanese Hatanaka army with about 1,000 men taken hostage Emperor Hiroito and imprisoned him in his palace; in the meantime the same Emperor had already fimato the act of unconditional surrender together with his military advisers and had engraved on two discs the speech to be done to the Nation.

Following the incursion of the flying fortresses B29 on Tokyo (other aircraft will continue to the city of Akita) the electricity was removed to the whole city and Major Hatanaka in the darkness can not find the discs where it was recorded the speech announcing the unconditional surrender of Japan to be announced on the radio on August 15, 1945.

Meanwhile, almost all of the B29 aircraft arrived on the Japanese city of Akita and dropped its bombs on the target (petrol depots and oil refinery), destroying 98% of the plant. The Head of Formation (who flew on plane B29 called Boomerang because he returned unharmed to the base after ten dangerous missions) gave orders to return to the base by communicating to the Strategic Air Command "Mission accomplished".

In Japan the conspirators will have gone through the guns or they will do Karakiri. During the re-formation the B29 formation will receive an "Apple" Radiotelegraphic message which meant that Japan had surrendered to the Americans without conditions.

The Second World War could be considered finished.

## Consolidated B-32 Dominator

The Consolidated B-32 Dominator was a strategic bomber, a four-engine propeller and a high wing, developed by the US aeronautics company Consolidated Aircraft Corporation in the early forties.

Produced starting from 1942 and destined to replace the previous B-24 Liberator, the B-32 was also conceived to be the 'spare wheel' of the USAF, in the event of failure of the technologically advanced, but also risky, program that was lead to the production of the B-29 Superfortress.

Compared to the latter, the B-32 was a less sophisticated aircraft, with a not very innovative design that made it similar to the previous B-24, despite being greatly enlarged and enhanced, and equipped with a single drift, as in the case of Consolidated PB4Y-2 Privateer.

Built in only 115 specimens, it was not very successful in the few war operations of the Second World War in which it took part, proving to be a tough opponent for Japanese fighters, but also dangerously subject to fatal accidents. Despite the flaws, the B-32 was still, in the field of World War II aircraft, a model second only in power to the B-29 and with characteristics very similar to it. Consolidated initially chose the Terminator name, but in August 1944 the Technical Subcommittee on naming aircraft proposed to change it into Dominator, a choice accepted by Consolidated. Later in the summer of 1945, the Assistant Secretary of State Archibald Mac Leish criticized the name as being unfit for an American aircraft, for which he returned to the Terminator name just before the cancellation of the program.

Like the other airplanes produced at that time, the B-32s were delivered unpainted apart from the antireflection panel above the nose in front of the cab and the engine covers on the inner sides that were dark olive FS34087 to prevent the reflections of the sun on the metal surfaces they could dazzle the crew; arrived at the department they were eventually camouflaged at the discretion of the commander.

# History

The project of the B-29 Superfortress began in mid-1938. In June 1940, USAAF asked the Consolidated alternative project as a reserve in case of problems in the development of the B-29. Consolidated proposed the Model 33 derived from the B-24, a similar project even if larger, and as the B-24 was characterized by the Davis wing with high elongation, an empennage with two disk drifts and doors of the hold bombs sliding, but the fuselage was larger, circular in section, and the snout was rounded. For the propulsion were provided engines Wright R-3350 Super Cyclone 2,200 hp with propellers Curtiss Electric tripala, the same as the B-

107

29, pressurized cabin and a defensive armament based on fourteen Browning M2 12.7 mm machine guns in remote controlled towers, all for the total weight expected of 45.814 kg. The USAAF signed a contract for three XB-32 prototypes on 6 September 1940, the same day of the order for the Boeing XB-29 prototype.

The first XB-32 number 41-141, was built in the Forth Worth Consolidated plant in Texas and flew for the first time on 7 September 1942. This first prototype was devoid of the pressurization system, the defensive towers and the trolley doors because they still gave some problems. The prototype had engines R-3350-13 to internal gondolas and R-3350-21 to external gondolas. The propellers of the internal engines had the possibility of inversion of the wheelbase to reduce the landing stroke. During the flight test phase the engines gave problems due to oil leakage and inadequate cooling.

The XB-32 "41-141" was equipped with eight 12.7 mm machine guns in two dorsal turrets and two ventral ones plus two 12.7 mm machine guns and a 20 mm cannon in each outer backward gondola remote controlled and a 12.7 mm machine gun in each wing outside the propellers, for a total of 20 machine guns.

On March 17, 1943, USAAF signed a supply contract for three hundred B-32s, although the prototype problems continued. On May 10, 1943, the first XB-32 crashed after taking thirty test flights due to a fault in the hypersupporters; on July 2, 1943, the second XB-32, number 41-142, flew for the first time. After some tests the USAAF requested a revision of the initial project that would have had to adopt numerous modifications, including a subdivision of the more traditional defensive armament due to problems with remote-controlled turrets. As a result, the number of 12.7 mm M2 machine guns was reduced to ten, divided as follows:
- Two in a Sperry A-17 front tower.
- Two in a Martin A-18 dorsal tower behind the cab.
- Two in a Martin A-18 dorsal tower in front of the drift.
- Two in a retractable Sperry ventral turret.
- Two in a caudal Sperry A-17 turret.

The problems related to the pressurization system were never solved, so it was decided to eliminate it for standard aircraft and not to use them at high altitudes.

The war load was increased from 1,814 kg to 9,072 kg, and a new system for pointing and unhooking the bombs and new four-blade propellers was introduced.

The second XB-32 continued to have stability problems, and, to solve them, after the twenty-fifth flight a single-drift tail similar to that of the B-29 was mounted, but without results.

The third XB-32, number 41-18336, flew for the first time on 3 November 1943 with a newly designed tail with 5.9 meters high drift.

## Use

Initially, the USAAF considered the B-32 to be a reserve project in the event of delays or bankruptcy of the B-29, but the success of the B-29 and program delays rendered the B-32 no longer necessary.

USAAF's plans to re-equip the Eighth and Fifteenth Air Force flight groups prior to their relocation to the Pacific were made impossible by the delivery of only five B-32s by the end of 1944, while the B- 29 was already in full production and use by the Twelfth Air Force. The delivery of the first B-32s began when General George Kenney, commander of the Fifth Air Force and allied air forces in the Southwest Pacific, went to Washington to request B-29s.

Since for the B-29 the priority was the strategic bombing the request was rejected, so Kenney asked the B-32s. Kenney was authorized to test the new planes in royal missions, so he was called a series of test missions and a plan to re-equip with the B-32 two of the four squadrons of the 312th Bomb Group, at the time all on Douglas A-20 Havoc.

On May 12, 1945, three B-32s departed from Forth Worth to the Clark Field base on the island of Luzon in the Philippines, where two arrived on the 24th and the third on the 25th, and were assigned to the 386th Bomb Squadron of the 312th Bomb Group for a a series of eleven test missions completed on 17 June. The crews were positively impressed by the short landing performance possible thanks to the Davis wing and the propeller pitch reversers on the internal engines. They also found several faults: the cabin was very noisy, the layout of the equipment unsuitable, the view of the bomber limited; also the plane was very heavy and the fires on the engines were frequent.

- On 29 May 1945 the B-32s carried out the first bombing mission against a supply depot at Antatet on the island of Luzon in the Philippines.
- On June 15, two B-32s dropped sixteen 907 kg bombs on a sugar refinery in Taito on the island of Taiwan.
- On 22 June, a B-32 attacked an alcohol distillery in Heito on the island of Taiwan with 227 kg bombs, on the same day another B-32 failed with 118 kg fragmentation bombs from anti-aircraft artillery posts.
- On June 25, the last bridge attack mission was carried out at Kiirun on the island of Taiwan.

The test missions were judged to be positive overall, so in the following July the 386th Bomb Squadron completed the transition on the B-32 and accomplished another six missions before the end of the war.

On August 13, the 386th Bomb Squadron was transferred to the Yontan Air Base, near Yomitan on the island of Okinawa, to perform photo reconnaissance missions to verify that Japanese surrender conditions were met. In the following days, another six B-32s arrived. During one of these missions, the B-32 were attacked, on August 17, by anti-aircraft and Japanese fighters, claiming a certain and two probable slaughter. On August 18, a formation of four Mitsubishi A6M "Zero" and three Kawanishi N1K2-J Shiden-Kai attacked four B-32s engaged in photographic reconnaissance missions to Japan; this was the last air combat of the war.

The B-32 number 42-108532 "Hobo Queen II" was severely damaged, one of the camera operators was wounded and another killed, the last victim in World War II combat among the allies. His crew claimed the demolition of two Zero and the probable abatement of a

Shiden-Kai. The last photographic recognition mission was performed on August 28th; on the same day two B-32s were destroyed in two different incidents that caused the death of fifteen of the twenty-six crewmen. The 386th Bomb Squadron finished operations on August 30th. The production of the B-32, of which another 1,598 were already ordered, was canceled on 8 September 1945 and ended on 12 October.

Consolidated TB-32 Dominator assembly line in Fort Worth, Texas.

All the B-32s were set aside at the Aerospace Maintenance And Regeneration Center (AMARC) on the Davis-Monthan Air Force Base in Arizona and subsequently scrapped, the last, number 42-108474 initially intended for the National Museum of the United States Air Force near the Wright-Patterson Air Force Base in Ohio, it was declared surplus and demolished in Davis-Monthan in August 1949.

## Versions

- XB-32 - Three prototypes used for test flights during project development.
- B-32A - Bombardment standard version. The first serial B-32, number 42-108471, was delivered to the USAAF on September 19, 1944 with a similar drift to the B-29. The same day he had an accident in landing due to failure of the front carriage. 75 aircraft of this version were produced.
- TB-32 - Disarmed training version with simplified avionics. It had about 320 kg of ballast distributed to maintain the center of gravity. The first TB-32A was delivered on January 27, 1945. 40 aircraft of this version were produced after the first fourteen B-32As.

**Technical features**

**Dimensions and weights**

- Crew: 10 men
- Length: 25.03 meters
- Wing span: 41.16 meters
- Height: 9.81 meters
- Wing area: 132.20 m2
- Empty weight: 27,400 kg
- Load weight: 45,722 Kg
- Maximum takeoff weight: 56,023 Kg
- Exemplary products: 118, of which:
  - 3 copies of XB-32
  - 75 copies of B-32
  - 40 TB-32 specimens

**Propulsion**

- Engine: 4 radial Wright R-3350-23A turbochargers
- Power: 2,200 hp (1,641 kW) each

**Performance**

- Maximum speed: 575 km / h to 9,150 meters
- Cruising speed: 467 km / h
- Ascent speed: 5.3 m / sec
- Autonomy: 6,118 km
- Tangency: 9,360 meters

## Armament

- Machine guns: 10 Browning M2 12.7 caliber
- Bombs: 9,100 kg

## Boeing B-50 Superfortress

The Boeing B-50 Superfortress was a four-engine strategic bomber, USA, developed after the Second World War as an evolution of the Boeing B-29 Superfortress, whose project was modified by replacing the engines with the most powerful radials Pratt & Whitney R-4360, a reinforced structure, higher tail rudder and other improvements. It was the last piston engine bomber designed by Boeing for the United States Air Force with which it remained in service for almost twenty years.

The development of an improved version of the B-29 began in 1944 with the aim of replacing the unreliable Wright R-3350 engines with the most powerful 28-cylinder four-row Pratt & Whitney R-4360 Wasp-Major radials.

A B-29A-5-BN, named XB-44 Superfortress, serial number 42-93845, was modified by Pratt & Whitney as a test bench for the installation of R-4360-33 engines of 3,000 Hp (2,240 kW), to replace the four 2,200 Hp R-3350s (1,640 kW) and made the first flight in May 1945.

The expected B-29D, equipped with the most powerful Wasp-Major engines, would have to incorporate further major changes beyond the proven engines with the B-44. Among these, the use of a new aluminum alloy, the 75-S, in place of the previously used 24ST. The new alloy would have allowed the construction of stronger and at the same time light wings. The landing gear would have been reinforced to support weights up to 18,200 kg greater than the B-29. There was also a larger vertical rudder, foldable to allow access to existing hangars and increased flaps necessary for the greater overall weight of the aircraft. The armament was similar to that of the B-29, consisting of two bombs capable of transporting a total of 9,100 kg of bombs plus an additional 3,600 kg externally loaded. The defensive armament consisted of 13 12.7 mm caliber machine guns and 12 machine guns and a 20 mm caliber cannon in five turrets.

An order for 200 B-29D was issued in June 1945, but the end of the Second World War in August 1945 led to the mass cancellation of all orders for military supplies, including the order for 5,000 B-29 canceled in September 1945 In December of the same year, the order for the B-29D was cut from 200 to 60 copies and at the same time the designation of the aircraft changed to B-50.

**Use**

Boeing built 370 B-50s divided between various models and variants in the period between 1947 and 1953, with the tanker and meteorological reconnaissance versions that remained in service until 1965. The first B-50A were delivered in June 1948 to the 43d Bombardment Wing of the Strategic Air Command, based at Davis-Monthan AFB in Arizona. The B-50As were also delivered to the 2d Bombardment Wing with Chatham AFB base in Georgia, while the 93d Bombardment Wing of Castle AFB in California and the 509th Bombardment Wing of Walker AFB in New Mexico were equipped with the B-50Ds later in 1949. The fifth and last flock of the SAC to receive the B-50D was the 97th Bombardment Wing based at Biggs AFB, Texas in December 1950. The mission assigned to these bombing flocks included the ability to drop atomic bombs on enemy targets, receiving orders directly from the President of the United States.

The 301st Bombardment Wing of MacDill AFB in Florida received some B-50A reassigned by Davis-Monthan at the beginning of 1951, but used them only for training, waiting to receive the B-47A Stratojet in June 1951. It was, in fact, planned that the B-50 would be the only interim strategic bomber awaiting the introduction of the B-47 Stratojet. The delays, however, of the latter model, forced the B-50 to prolong the stay in service in the SAC for all the fifties. In 1949, a strategic reconnaissance version of the B-50B, the RB-50, was developed to replace the old RB-29s used by the SAC in intelligence operations against the then Soviet Union. There were three different configurations produced, which were later redesigned RB-50E, RB-50F and RG-50G.

- The RB-50E was specialized in photographic recognition and observation missions.
- The RB-50F resembled the RB-50E, but embarked the SHORAN navigation radar system designed to conduct cartographic and geodetic measurement campaigns.
- RB-50G specialized in electronic recognition.

These aircraft were mainly in service with the 55th Strategic Reconnaissance Wing; RB-50E were also used by the 91st Strategic Reconnaissance Wing as replacement for RB-29 photographic reconnaissance on North Korea during the Korean War.

The vast northern borders of the Soviet Union were completely unguarded in many parts at the beginning of the Cold War, with little radar coverage and little ability to target detection. The 55th SRW RB-50s flew many missions along these boundaries and sometimes, when necessary, even within Soviet airspace; at the beginning there was little opposition due to insufficient radar coverage and in any case, even in case of discovery of the intrusion, the Soviet fighter planes of the time, technologically stopped at the Second World War, were not able to intercept the RB- 50 at high altitudes where they operated.

The entry into service of the MiG-15 interceptors in the early 1950s made the overly dangerous trespassing operations and there were some Superfortess knocked down with the wrecks examined by Soviet spy experts. The RB-50 missions on the territory of the Soviet Union ended in 1954, when the aircraft was replaced by the RB-47 Stratojet able to fly at even higher altitudes and with almost supersonic speeds.

The B-47 Stratojet was produced in large numbers since 1953 and ended up replacing the B-50D of the SAC in service with the last Superfortess withdrawn in 1955. After the employment with the SAC, a large number of aircraft was modified and turned into tankers assuming the denomination KB-50, or were converted as aircraft for meteorological recognition assuming the name WB-50 and passed on to the Air Weather Service. The KB-50s, with their engines superior to that of the KB-29s used in Tactical Air Command, proved to be more suited to the task of fueling jet-powered tactical fighters, such as the F-100 Super Saber. KB-50 and later KB-50J with J-47 jet engines, were used by the TAC and also by the USAFE and PACAF in the role of suppliers. Some were dislocated in Thailand and carried out refueling missions in the skies of Indochina in the early years of the Vietnam War, until they were withdrawn from service in March 1965 due to the discovery of metal fatigue and corrosion phenomena identified during the investigations on KB-50J, number 48-065, crashed on October 14, 1964.

In addition to the conversion into the tanker, there was the one to meet the needs of the Air Weather Service which in 1955 had practically exhausted the ability to continue to fly its own fleet of WB-29 hurricane hunting and other reconnaissance missions weather. Thirty-six B-50D of the SAC were disarmed and equipped with long-range meteorological radars and renamed WB-50. These aircraft could fly higher and faster than the previous WB-29 and they played an important role in the Cuban missile crisis, when they kept under control the meteorological situation around Cuba in order to be able to plan the photographic reconnaissance missions.

Although missions for meteorological studies are considered as peacetime missions, the dangerous hurricane hunt paid a high tribute to victims, with 66 aviators missing due to the 13 incidents that involved the WB-50s during their career. ten years. Also for these aircraft the withdrawal from the service was decreed in 1965 after the results of the investigation on KB-50J that led to the discovery of the phenomena of structural failure and corrosion on the cells. No B-50 remains in flight conditions today, although some specimens are kept in museums exhibited static.

**Technical features**

**Dimensions and weights**

- Crew: 11 men
- Length: 30.20 meters
- Wing opening: 43.10 meters
- Height: 9.75 meters
- Wing area: 160 m2
- Empty weight: 36,800 Kg
- Maximum takeoff weight: 76,560 Kg
- Exemplary products: about 400

**Propulsion**

- Engine: 4 radial Pratt & Whitney R-4360 radial turbochargers with 28 cylinders
- Power: 3,500 hp (2,240 kW) each

**Performance**

- Maximum speed: 620 km / h
- Autonomy: 7,600 km
- Tangency: 11,200 meters

**Armament**

- Machine guns: 10 Browning M2 12.7 caliber
- Cannons: 1 of 20 mm
- Bombs: up to 12,720 kg

## Convair B-36

The Convair B-36 between 1947 and 1958 was the intercontinental bomber par excellence in strength of the US Strategic Air Command. Although he never received an official name, he was nicknamed Peacemaker (pacifier) based on the proposal put forward by Convair, following a competition launched among company employees to find a name for the aircraft. The crews instead dubbed him Magnesium Overcast.

The B-36 is the largest bombing aircraft ever built, with its 6 3,600 hp engines and the subsequent addition of 4 turbojets. It remained in service until 1958, when its performance was overcome by both jet fighters and the new generation of bombers, such as the B-52. The Convair B-36 was the result of a specification of the United States Army Air Corps, dating back to 1941: at the time, faced with the possibility that Germany would occupy the United Kingdom, the US authorities requested an intercontinental bomber with which they could to hit the enemy starting from the bases in the mother country. The specification in question provided for an aircraft capable of carrying over 4,500 kg of bombs at around 5,500 km and flying over 480 km / h to a maximum height of 10,760 meters.

At the end of the selection, among various proposals, the choice of USAAC awarded Model 37 of the Consolidated Aircraft Corporation, which would later be merged into Convair: on November 15, 1941, USAAC signed the order for two XB-36 designated prototypes.

It was the project of a mammoth plane, which presented the unusual configuration with six engines arranged in a thrusting position, double-sided fletching, taken from the B-24, and cockpit not protruding from the diameter of the fuselage, as for the Boeing B-29. Even before seeing the light, the project was subjected to several modifications, among which the main one concerned the tail plans that acquired the final configuration with the single drift at the end of the fuselage.

The first completed prototype left the factory on September 8, 1945, but it took 11 months before it could make the first flight, August 8, 1946. The first flight tests were satisfactory, even though they highlighted the poor visibility from the cockpit that in the second example it was raised and equipped with a bubble roof. Among other changes decided after the first tests, the installation of a post at the extreme bow for a machine gunner (two machine guns). The first samples of the series were delivered to the departments in August 1948, while the production of the B-36B version which had a complete defensive armament, consisting of 16 20-mm cannons housed in pairs in eight turrets, had just begun. fore and a tail while the others were arranged along the fuselage in remote control and retractable locations, using sliding doors.

In 1947, a transport aircraft developed by the B-36 project was proposed: an aircraft of enormous size, larger than a

Boeing 747, with the redesigned fuselage and equipped with a double bridge for 410 fully equipped soldiers or, in hospital version, 300 wounded. After the initial interest of American Airlines, the XC-99, as the aircraft was named, had no production developments and the prototype was used by the USAF as a transport until 1957.

The XB-36 prototype next to a B-29.

The search for higher and higher propulsive powers proved to be decisive for the development of the B-36: first it was proposed a version with engines in the most classic propeller-driven configuration, discarded, then the engines already used were upgraded, which went from 3,000 to 3,500 hp. Lastly, a B-36B was equipped with turbojet engines installed in pairs in gondolas under the wings. The engines installed were initially four Allison J35, soon replaced by as many General Electric J47 that developed 23.05 kN. Based on improved performance, all pre-existing aircraft were adjusted to this standard.

The next step was a modified project that, while re-proposing the original fuselage, featured arrow wings and motorisation exclusively with turbojet with 8 Pratt & Whitney J57 arranged in 4 coupled gondolas attached to the wings. This aircraft, initially referred to as B-36G, flew in April 1952 but was soon redesigned YB-60; presented in response to the specification that would have led to the successor of the B-36, it was outclassed by the Boeing B-52 Stratofortress.

The development of the B-36 cell had therefore matured; the later versions, the main part of the production of the aircraft, were characterized by refinements of the project: first the radar equipment and internal systems were improved (B-36H) then tanks were installed in the outer wing trunks and the landing gear was strengthened (B - 36J).

Other versions were built in relation to the special projects designed by the Strategic Air Command of the USAF.

The B-36, considering all the versions produced, was in service with the Strategic Air Command of the United States Air Force between 1948 and 1958. The bases from which it operated in the various departments were all on the American continent and in Puerto Rico although, with a certain frequency, they were risked abroad, especially in Great Britain.

The first department equipped with the Peacemaker was the 7th Bombardment Wing, operating in the Carswell AFB, near Fort Worth, Texas; on the opposite side of the airport the establishments of the Convair were located. During its operational life the B-36 was never used in war operations, but its name will remain linked to several experimental projects that saw him engaged for a long time. Among other noteworthy events there were certainly two incidents involving aircraft that were operating with a nuclear bomb on board, a definite event, in code, Broken Arrow. The first of these took place on 13 February 1950 when the crew of the B-36B, serial number 44-92075, was forced to abandon the aircraft following a fire to engines off British Columbia: the bomb, a Mk 4 unarmed bomb, was dropped by the crew before leaving the plane. In the second case, on 22 May 1957 the crew of a B-36 accidentally dropped a hydrogen bomb "Mark 17" in a deserted area before landing at Kirtland AFB in Albuquerque, New Mexico. Also in this case the bomb was not armed and there was only the explosion of the conventional explosive. Both these incidents remained secretly covered for decades.

The B-36 was a large high wing monoplane, with a circular section fuselage. The internal volume was about $510 \text{ m}^3$ and even in the wings there were tunnels, which allowed the maintenance of the engines, over 2.10 meters high; in this way it could be accessed in an upright position. The height of the vertical tail, 14.22 meters, often forced to keep the tail outside the hangars. The six piston engines that powered the Peacemaker since the original design were the radials Pratt & Whitney R-4360. These large 28-cylinder engines, arranged over 4 stars, were the most powerful stellar engine ever produced for aviation.

The engines were placed in a thrusting position, even if this arrangement caused some problems: the design of the engines was carried out for the most common tractor position and in particular the carburetors were expected to be heated, above all at higher altitudes, by the air flow coming from the cylinders. In this case the flow of air directly hit the carburetors, without any possibility of heating them. In particular, in the presence of humidity, the formation of ice in the air intakes of the carburettors risked, which, by modifying the composition of the air / fuel mixture, led to an increase in the production of unburnt gases, which in turn could suddenly ignite. to determine, in extreme cases, the loss of the aircraft.

Starting from the B-36D version to the piston engines the use of turbojet was added: two pairs of General Electric J47 engines were installed in a sub-machine gondola located in the external part of each half-wing, which guaranteed a significant increase in the performance of the aircraft , in terms of speed and load capacity.

Divided into four bombs, the B-36 was able to transport 21,000 kg of bombs normally, but it was possible, by reducing the operating autonomy, to transport up to 39,000 kg; it was more than 10 times the possibilities of a B-17.

The B-36 was not designed as a nuclear bomber, if only because, at the time, these weapons were but a project; in any case, the B-36 assumed that role as soon as it entered service and remained the only means capable of unhooking the large Mark-17 hydrogen bombs until the B-52 entered service. In flights involving the use of such bombs it was necessary to unify two adjacent bombs. The defensive armament consisted of 16 20 mm automatic cannons arranged in 8 turrets: six were arranged in fuselage, four dorsals and two ventral ones, in retractable positions, while the remaining two were fixed and placed at the ends of the aircraft.

**Technical features**

**Dimensions and weights**

- Crew: 13 men
- Length: 49.40 meters
- Wing opening: 70.10 meters
- Height: 14.22 meters
- Wing area: 443.32 m$^2$
- Empty weight: 77,581 Kg
- Load weight: 119,318 Kg
- Maximum takeoff weight: 185,976 Kg
- Exemplary products: 384

**Propulsion**

- Engine: 6 radial Pratt & Whitney R-4360-53 with 4 General Electric J47 turbojet
- Thrust: 2.8 kN each radial and 24 kN each turbojet

**Performance**

- Maximum speed: 672 km / h at high altitude
- Cruising speed: 370 km / h
- Ascent speed: 10.1 m / s
- Autonomy: 16,000 km
- Range of action: 6,415 km
- Tangency: 13,300 meters

**Armament**

- Cannons: 8 turrets, of which 6 retractable inside the fuselage, armed with two retractable Hispano-Suiza HS.404 20 mm cannons.
- Bombs: up to 39,000 kg

Printed in Great Britain
by Amazon